GOLD IN THE RIVER

GOLD IN THE RIVER

TRUE STORIES FROM THE LIFE OF AN ORDINARY WOMAN

JOYCE FENTON WHITE

To Irene & Don
with love from
Joyce x
Be blessed as
you read!

DEDICATION

This book is dedicated to my wonderful husband Bob, my four children, Pauline, David, Andrew and Jonathan through whom I have learnt much about depending on God. Also to my grandchildren Darren, Christopher, Emma, Ruth and Sarah and my great grandchildren Khye, Mya, Libby Mae and Charlotte that they all may know and love for themselves the God I know and trust.

Let each generation tell its children of your mighty acts; let them proclaim your power.
(Psalm 145 verse 4)

CONTENTS

FOREWORD

"Gold in the River" is a testimony from an ordinary person, Joyce White, and her interactions with an Extraordinary God. It is an encouragement to us all to step out in faith and trust in the Living God. She magnificently reflects on the power of prayer to guide, to heal, and to comfort. Her family, friends and readers will appreciate this woman of God and her journey of faith.
Rev. Graham Timson, Peterborough, December 2019

PREFACE

I always wanted to write. My dream as a young person would have been to be a journalist, or a writer. I loved reading and always in my head would be outlines of stories, which never got onto paper. However at this late stage in my life, I had begun sharing some of these 'God stories' verbally with people and many commented, you ought to write them down. I became increasingly aware that when I depart this life, unless they are written, they would die with me and even my own family would not necessarily know about them.

And so I started writing them down, praying for guidance as to which ones to write. They were written in no particular order, just as they came to mind. Most of them have been written during 2019. I was then unsure as to how to put them together, because they cover a time span of some fifty plus years of my Christian life, during two marriages, and living in some four locations and at seven different addresses. So in order for them to make a little sense, I decided to put them into loosely chronological order and that involved writing some 'link' stories.

They were intended to be standalone stories, so that each is entire in itself and can be read separately, but as a whole they give a little glimpse into my relationship with the God of the Universe. This book is not in any sense my memoirs, which if written would be an entirely different story. As I have said at the end, the Bible says that if everything that Jesus did could be written into books, even the whole world could not contain them. There are many things which He is still doing today and if this small offering encourages other people to write their own stories then my mission will be accomplished.

Joyce Fenton White
Solihull - February 2020

ACKNOWLEDGE-MENTS

I would like to thank my friends Mike and Pam Holt for their encouragement without which this book may not have been written and especially Mike for his prophetic and editing input also my friends in Jubilee Church Life Group for their encouragement and prophetic input, namely Deepak and Rebecca (not forgetting Joel!), Rosie, Andrea, Mary and Sally.

A special thanks also to Pauline and Desmond

for their critical appraisal and constructive suggestions.

Many thanks also to Professor Wayne P. Armstrong of Palomar College California for giving me permission to use his photograph on the cover of my book.

INTRODUCTION

"There's gold in them thar hills!" so goes the well-known saying.

There are many rivers in the world where gold can be found and recently there has been renewed interest in panning for gold following the discovery of a nugget worth £50,000 in an undisclosed river in Scotland. (*Wikipedia*)

Panning for gold consists of scooping grit and mud from the riverbed into a special pan and shaking or rocking it from side to side with a motion that would cause any gold which is heavier than the material around it to sink to the bottom of the pan.

Any gold may be so small as to be almost invisible to the naked eye, just tiny specks, but there is always the hope that those who have spent long hours in the cold and rain may discover some larger ones or even some which may be termed 'nuggets'.

It is this which has inspired the title of this book. In the ordinariness of the river of life, through the grit and mire of the everyday, if we are looking for it through the sifting and shaking and nitty gritty of our lives, we may find some glimpses of gold and even a few choice nuggets.

Most of life is made up of getting up in the morning, eating cornflakes or our favourite cereal, tending families, taking the kids to school, cleaning the house, going to work; the humdrum routine of the mundane …..but now and then the miraculous breaks into the mundane, heaven touches earth, the supernatural is superimposed on the natural and the extraordinary invades the ordinary.

In this book, I am recounting a few of those true stories from my own life experience. Those glittering touches of the gold of heaven flowing through the river of life if we will only search for them…….

ANDREW'S HEALING

A figure emerged from the kitchen at Castlerigg camp bearing a cake with 18 candles and a chunk of Lake District slate. It was my twins Andrew and Jonathan's birthday and the slate with a miniature figure of a climber signified that Andrew had just climbed Scafell Pike, the highest mountain in England, for the first time.

The slim, blond, curly-headed young man who was my son Andrew blew out the candles. 18!!! They had grown up so fast. It was 1983, the year Bob and I had been married, three and a half years after the death of my first husband John, the father of my children.

Four years earlier, just one month before his sudden death, we had been at the same camp for the tenth year, but I had sensed from God that was to be our last holiday there together as a family. I had never expected to return, but the church Bob and I were now attending decided to go there together, so they persuaded us to go along too.

It was a happy, but also for me a bitter-sweet occasion because there were so many memories. But now I had a new husband and the future looked bright as we were beginning our new life together. Little did we know what lay ahead in the coming months.........

The following April, just a week or so after Bob and I celebrated our first wedding anniversary, one by one each of my four children went down with some kind of 'flu' bug, temperatures, etc. Andrew was the last to succumb – he was never ill, never took time out from school or work and in spite of feeling unwell, he really didn't want to stay home. Under pressure, he did.

When the temperature hadn't gone down after a week, I took him to the doctor, who sent him to the hospital for a blood test.

The next day, late in the evening, the doctor called round unexpectedly. Said he wanted him in hospital straight away and used our phone to arrange for him to be admitted. There was a problem with his white blood cell count. I thought it was strange that he said to the person on the other end of the line, "His father and grandfather both died suddenly, I'd like you to do what you can for him."

We took him to the hospital where a doctor examined him and said "It's probably glandular fever. Nothing to worry about, but we'll keep him in as a precaution."

After being admitted they decided that his white blood cell count was so low his immune system would not be able to resist infection so they transferred him to the isolation unit at another hospital. Usually that unit protected other people from infected patients, but Andrew was isolated to protect HIM from any infection. He had a biopsy taken from a lump on his neck, but because it was Easter, the lab result was not available for a week.

Meanwhile, to protect him, all windows had to be kept closed to prevent any airborne germs invading the room and visitors had to wear gowns, masks and shoe covers which was unbearable in an exceptionally hot spell.

After a week, I was called to the Doctor's office who broke the news to me, "It's Hodgkin's Disease which is a blood cancer, but not to worry, it's easily treatable at this hospital."

I went home to tell Bob, hardly reassured. We put out requests for prayer to everyone we knew in a number of different churches.

Shortly afterwards, we were again called to the

Doctor's office.

"I'm afraid it's more advanced than we had thought, so we need to send him to London, to Hammersmith Hospital, where there's just one man in England who may be able to help him."

Ouch! This was worse than we had ever imagined possible.

Andrew, Bob and I were taken to London in a sterilised ambulance; Bob and I with our clobber of gowns, masks, head and shoe covering. We walked into a big hospital ward looking like something from another planet to be greeted by the eminent man himself, Dr. John Goldman.

"You can take off all that," he said, indicating our spacemen-like gear. "We don't do that here but treat with antibiotics." He continued, "Don't worry, we should be able to treat him successfully".

Andrew was put in a bed in the open ward.

The next time we saw Dr. Goldman, he was a little less optimistic. "It's more advanced than I thought, but there is just a chance I might be able to do something for him." He was interested to learn that Andrew had a twin brother as there might be a possibility of a bone marrow transplant if they were compatible.

Chemotherapy was started, and I travelled

daily from Leigh-on-Sea to be with him. Then the rest of the family were complaining that they saw so little of me, so I would drive up to London one day and sleep in the day room adjoining the ward overnight and back the next morning. I did that on alternate days for two months spending one night at the hospital and the following one at home. The M25 had just been built as far as South Mimms so from there I would drop down into London learning all the back doubles and shortest routes possible to get to the hospital.

By June Andrew was no better, in fact he hardly got out of bed any more. The top man in his field in England, Dr. Goldman, did a ward round with his entourage, "I'm afraid he's not responding to the chemotherapy, there's nothing more I can do for him."

That day was the only one I had not driven myself to London, but the pastor of our church had taken me in his car. I cried all the way home.

"What are you crying about?" asked Colin. "It's no harder for God to heal cancer than to heal the common cold!"

"I know that but I don't like being put to the test on this one."

Bob and I went to our church home group that evening and it was suggested we ask God why this had happened to us. "I don't need to ask why, I trust God knows what he's doing."

I cried most of the night, gave Andrew completely into God's hands. "He's yours Lord, whether you choose to heal him or take him home to be with you," then I reached a place of peace and dozed a little till morning.

I was reminded of something I had read in a book by Catherine Marshall. She calls it 'the prayer of relinquishment'. She relates how she had been ill for a long time and specialists had not been able to help her and all prayer prayed in faith had failed to be answered. She came to a point of abject acceptance. "I'm tired of asking....I'm beaten, finished, God, You decide what You want for the rest of my life....." Tears flowed. She says "I had no faith as I understood faith. I expected nothing. The gift of my sick self was made with no trace of graciousness.

"The result was as if windows had opened in heaven; as if some Dynamo of heavenly power had begun flowing, flowing into me. From that moment my recovery began." (Beyond Ourselves by Catherine Marshall).

Next day I set off once again to Hammersmith Hospital and as soon as I walked into the ward, as usual the first thing I did was look at Andrew's temperature chart. His temperature had been doing wild swings for the last two months, extreme highs and lows.

IT HAD STABILISED OVERNIGHT DOWN TO THE NORMAL LINE!!!

The same medical team came round as had visited the day before. Beaming, we were told, "His spleen which was enlarged yesterday has come down to normal and his temperature is normal. He's starting to get better!"

A blood test confirmed this.

He was soon discharged home to continue with fortnightly trips to the hospital for chemo.

After some time I asked how they would know when the disease had gone. "Oh, it went away the day his spleen went down and his temperature normalised."

"Then why are you still treating him?" I asked.

"Just a precaution," was the reply. "To make sure it doesn't come back."

The hospital never said he was cured, only that it had 'gone into remission'. But we knew better ....and that's now 35 years ago.........

In the next chapter I'll wind back eighteen years to the beginning of my journey of faith...........

SISTER CHAMBERS

My sister Pat and I were both pregnant at the same time in 1965, but she was expecting her baby five weeks earlier than mine.

We used to waddle along to the clinic together to see the midwife. It was mainly because of this, I think, that the midwife queried whether I had my dates right …….by the height and size of my tum, I should have been due around the same time as my sister. I was positive about the dates.

"Any twins in your family?" she asked.

"No," I replied. So she wrote 'query multiple pregnancy' on my clinic card and sent me along to the doctor.

The doctor a week later examined me. "What's she talking about!" he laughed. "There's only one there, but in case there's a problem I'll send you to the gynaecologist."

Another week went by before I saw Mrs. Bridges. On examination, she pronounced, "There's definitely only one baby, but I'll send you for X-ray in case you're placenta praevia". This questioned whether the placenta was blocking the exit canal.

I duly attended the X-ray with two other girls who were both excitedly expecting to find they had twins because they both had twins in their families. I did not but I was only concerned to find if there was anything wrong. If I was placenta praevia it would mean delivery by Caesarian Section.

The three of us sat in the waiting room till the results came through.

The radiologist held up the X-ray plate........."Mrs. Fenton, you've got twins!!"

I was the only one of the three to be carrying twins.

That was five weeks before due date and they wanted to keep me in hospital so that I could rest. I refused because I had two year old David and three and a half year old Pauline to get home to.

I struggled on for another week, then following an exhausting walk to the clinic to see Mrs. Bridges again, who incidentally now on examination could find two babies quite easily, felt that walk was just the last straw and I went into labour that evening four weeks early.

It was August, and a hot and busy labour ward with twenty mothers all at various stages of delivery at the same time meant that I was left alone for a long time with only a bell to summon help if I needed it.

I was getting no pain so I didn't call anyone. Eventually, a nurse popped in and asked if anything was happening. This was so different from my two previous deliveries which had taken place at home and you had the constant attention of a dedicated midwife.

She felt my tum and said, "You're getting contractions, you just can't feel them. We'll tell you when to push and you'll just have to get on with it".

Andrew arrived first, followe 18 minutes later by his brother Jonathan. I remember hearing a phone ring outside the room just as Andrew came into the world. It was my husband John, who when he was told only one was born, wondered what had happened to the other one.

In theory in those days, if husbands wanted to be present at the birth they could, but in practice it was largely discouraged, usually by a suggestion that they go away and phone in periodically.

After some hours, although the twins were one

month premature, their weights were good at 5lb. 6oz. and 5lb. 14oz. so we were sent to an ordinary ward.

In our changeable English climate, though it was August, the weather changed and temperatures dropped, such that two little 'prem' babies couldn't adjust to the change and they had to be taken to the premature baby unit.

For two weeks I stayed in hospital to be near them but felt rather at a loose end in a ward where everyone else had a baby with them and I didn't. The normal length of time to stay in hospital was nine days. In addition, in those days, older children were not allowed to visit so I had not seen Pauline and David, my two older children for two weeks.

They were about to send me home alone, when they suddenly decided Jonathan could join me on the ward and they wanted me to stay in longer to get used to feeding him.

Things were looking up until Jonathan developed a rash. As a precaution we were put into isolation in a small room. I was feeling quite depressed and wondering if there was a God and if he cared about me.

Feeling quite weepy, I was surprised when the door opened and a nurse I hadn't seen before entered.

"I'm Sister Chambers," she announced. "What are you crying for? It's not like you to cry, you've been doing so well."

I told her my tale of woe and how much I was missing my other children at home.

"Well as it's Bank Holiday on Monday, as a special treat we're going to let them come to see you."

That cheered me up.

She asked about my twins names, Andrew James and Jonathan Mark. "Why have you chosen Bible names?" she asked.

Then she went on to talk about each of those people in the Bible just as though she knew each one of them personally. Certainly I had never known those things, they were just names in a book and although I had been a Sunday School teacher for years and taught Bible stories they had never come alive in the way that Sister Chambers talked about them. She knew the character of each of those people as though they were friends of hers.

There was something about this lady I couldn't quite put my finger on. I had never met anyone like her before. She told me that she belonged to a certain church in Leigh-on-Sea near to where I lived. And then she left the room.

I never saw her again. I was in hospital for a further week and Pauline and David were brought in to see me in that little tiny room on Bank Holiday Monday. Two-year-old David didn't remember me at all and clung to his dad, but Pauline climbed onto my bed and talked non-stop!

A week later I was discharged with Jonathan, while Andrew stayed in the premature baby unit and I was given instructions to phone on Mondays and Thursdays until he was ready to go home.

When I got home, where my mother who was registered blind had been looking after the other two children together with my husband, I found that she had been provided with a home help by the local social services. Mum had told me about her on a visit to the hospital. "You'll really like this lady! She's lovely".

And I did. I discovered that Joy was a Christian, not that she preached.....there was just something special about her, a peace that I couldn't describe, but it was something I wanted and set out to find.......

On one occasion I went along to the church that Sister Chambers had mentioned and tried to find her.........but no one there had ever heard of her.........

It's now August, 2019 and my twins will be 54 next week. Last night I woke in the night and for some unknown reason thought about these events that had eventually led to my meeting Jesus personally and finding he is still alive today doing the same things he did which are written in the Bible.

I remembered the conversation with the nursing sister who had visited me when I was in isolation in the hospital with Jonathan all those years ago and her almost uncanny knowledge of the characters whose names I had given to my sons and wondered for the first time........ could she have been an angel?

Last night, I just could not remember her name, then in the small hours, I remembered. Yes, it was Chambers. Was this significant? I don't know, but I got out of bed to look up Bible references to God's inner.chambers.

She certainly had come to me from God in a moment of my need and ministered to me in a way that led to my searching for Him.

All I know is that the Bible says that angels are sent as ministering spirits to those who are to inherit salvation.

We tend to think of angels as heavenly beings dressed in white with huge wings floating several feet above the ground, but that would be quite scary! The Bible has a number of stories of angels appearing as ordinary human beings. One day I shall know if Sister Chambers was one such......

FIRST STEPS

After leaving hospital with my newborn twins, life became extremely busy. Our little family had doubled overnight from two to four but more importantly the financial pressure with additional mouths to feed and needs to take care of was quite overwhelming.

I needed help!! "God if you're real, will you show me. I need help!" I also wondered if I were to die where I would go to.

I determined to go to all the churches in the town if necessary to find the answers I was looking for.

When the twins were about two months old I set off one Sunday evening on the start of my journey, deciding first of all to visit a big church near to my home. As I was passing a small chapel on the way up the road, I noticed it for the first time. It was a very ordinary looking building, almost indistinguishable from the bungalows around it which was probably why I had never consciously noticed it before. I changed my plan and turned in through the gate and entered the small building which was called a Gospel Hall. There I was greeted by some friendly faces and warmly shaken by the hand.

It had a warm, comfortable, homely feel and reminded me of my grandmother and a little chapel she used to take me to when I was a child. The hymns they sang were quite upbeat.

I returned the following week.........and the following week......

On my third visit, the preaching really made sense – I learned that the God I had been wondering about really cared about me. He was a loving Father who loved his creation so much that he had sent his only son Jesus into the world so that anyone who accepted him could come into his family and know the presence of his Spirit. After I got home that evening, I made the transaction. His life for mine. My desperate, difficult, life with all its failures and misery and shortcomings, for his glorious wholeness and provision. Wow.....what a trade-in......!!!!!

The difficulties remained, but the first thing I noticed was a desire to read the Bible. I only had an old children's bible given as a Sunday school prize and illustrated with pictures, and an old copy of the King James Version which had been given to my grandfather in the 1800s and passed down to me. In addition it really started to come alive and made sense. The bits (many) that I didn't understand, I asked God by his Spirit to show me what they meant, and he always did, in sometimes amazing and unexpected ways.

Another thing that constantly happened was that whenever the family had needs, such as for clothing or food, this always was provided. Sometimes bags of secondhand clothes were left on the doorstep and always were just what was needed.

While I was in hospital a lady came to me and offered me a twin pram. I gladly accepted.

I wanted to be 'Spirit-taught' – not just accept the norm which happened to be the 'done thing' generally. One of those norms was that 'Christians don't gamble'. But I wanted to know why. Surely there was no harm in the odd few pence on a Saturday evening to play cards?

John my husband would go shopping on Saturdays to buy our week's grocery supplies and then there was no more money until I got my family allowance on Tuesdays. My mother would often visit at the weekend and would give me two shillings (quite a lot of money in the 1960s! but now 10p in today's decimal coinage) to buy bread on Monday to feed the children. That was the only money I had in the world and when the in-laws came round to play cards on Saturday evenings I gambled it, ha'penny by ha'penny. I was uncomfortable with it, but "hey Joyce it's only ha'pennies!" they said.

And I would always win. So I got my two shillings back and sometimes a bit extra. This went on for weeks or maybe months. Until.........one disastrous evening, I lost!

Now I knew what it felt like for families where the dad would gamble away the families food money and they were unable to eat. The sense of guilt and shame that swept over me was overwhelming! No matter that father-in-law gave me his winnings "to buy sweets for the children". That money was no longer mine and there was no money to buy bread on Monday without stealing from the children which would add to my sense of guilt.

I had learned a serious lesson.

In 1969 Gwyn Jordan came to speak at the little chapel service one Sunday evening. I always liked listening to his preaching, but on this occasion he recounted and showed slides of a family camp in the Lake District at Castlerigg just outside Keswick. As it was a family camp I longed to be able to go there as a family.......but could we manage it financially?

"Lord if this is your will, then please provide for us all to go...!"

I did outwork, machining pre-cut purses, or sometimes addressing envelopes by hand which might earn the princely sum of sixpence an hour (two and a half pence in decimalised money). I saved as much as I could but then the children would need shoes and down the savings would go. By the time we set off for the fourteen hour coach journey from Leigh-on-Sea to Keswick, we had only just got enough for the quoted price of the camp for the six of us. Not a penny for spending money. Everything was paid in cash in those days, we had no bank account.

We arrived on Saturday and on Monday morning everyone queued up to pay their dues. I handed over my precious savings. To my amazement, they handed back to us some of it saying, "We won't charge for the children!" Wow! We now had a little spending money.

Our accommodation was in what looked like a garden shed with three sets of bunks in it and a sack over the broken window to keep out the draught! ....But it might have been the Ritz I was so praising God that we were able to be there – and he had made the impossible possible. The Bible says that he will provide all our needs and he always does......!

IF YOU ASK ANYTHING

D oris was dying. She was a lady we had known in the Congregational church my sister and I had attended when we were children. She was in charge of the primary department of the Sunday school. I was and had been all my life, a nominal churchgoer. At the age of 15, under the guidance of Doris, I had become a Sunday School teacher, first in the primary department, then going on to teach older children. I knew the bible stories ....but I didn't know the author of them.

Moving on, I became aware of a lack in my life and often wondered if I were to die, where I would go. I really wanted to know if God was real and if he was more than a collection of stories in a book.

Through many difficulties in my life, by the time my twins were born in 1965, I was really looking for answers. At that time a number of people entered my life who seemed to have a peace about them that I didn't have. Two of these were Sister Chambers and Joy Barker whom I have mentioned in a previous chapter.

One Sunday evening when my twins were about two months old, I set off up the road to a little chapel I had only recently noticed. There I heard for the first time, that Jesus came into the world to make it possible for mankind to go to live in heaven for eternity. I remembered my grand-mother who almost as soon as I had learned to talk, taught me the Bible verse that says, 'God so loved the world, that he gave his only son, that whoever believes in Him should not perish, but have eternal life.' Only by his death he opened the way. One more step, I knelt by my bed and asked this Jesus to come into my life and take control of it. I had known the teaching all my life, but hadn't known the reality and that he is still alive today by his spirit, doing miracles and giving people new life. Finding people like me who were lost, saving us from the consequences of a messed up life.

Pauline at four years old was still attending the Congregational Sunday School, being taught by Christine, Doris' daughter, and her friend Lindsay. In my early teaching days I had taught Christine.

Christine and Lindsay came round to visit

.....how was I to tell them that my life had been a phoney, my life had just been an outward expression of piety with no reality?

But they had something to share with me! As we all sat in the garden on a lovely summer's day, they told a similar story – both of them had recently invited Jesus into their lives!

I then told them of my journey, how I now also had had that personal encounter with the King of the universe and he was now in my life.

Excitedly, they both declared, "That's wonderful, but we didn't know that you weren't a Christian already".

I now attended the little chapel close to my home, but apart from regular Sunday services, I had very little contact with other Christians. In my hunger to know more about this living God in my life, I devoured the Bible in whole chunks. It really came alive!

About three years after my initial experience with God my mother gave me a new Bible still the King James Authorised version but which had cross references, so I went back and forth from the New to the Old Testament to learn the context of the teaching.

Nobody told me that the things that happened in the Bible were not for today, so I believed it when I read that Jesus is the same, yesterday, today and forever.

Therefore when I heard that Doris was dying with cancer, while sitting at my desk in an office doing some temporary work for the firm of estate agents I used to work for, I asked this Jesus, who was unchangingly the same, and who answered requests that were according to his will, to please heal Doris.

At that time there was a considerable spiritual awakening.

People like me were becoming aware of the reality of God, and his Spirit was bringing them to life. This was causing some disruption in the churches where people had been content with the outward religiosity without the reality.

Those of us who knew Him in this way started to meet together for discussion and worship. At one of these meetings I learned that there had been something of a miracle. Many people were praying for Doris, but it appeared that at the very time I was in my office asking for her healing and return from her deathbed, that Doris had sat up in bed, got out and knew that strength had come into her.

Many times after that I heard her testify about the amazing recovery – I never told anyone about my experience on that day.

PUTTING OUT
A FLEECE

There was quite a buzz of excitement around my circle of friends because we had heard there was to be a new centre and coffee bar for outreach to drug addicts and people with problems in the centre of Southend. It was to be called the OJ Centre, which stood for Operation Jerusalem a name taken from the New Testament which said that the gospel would be preached first of all in Jerusalem, then in Samaria then in the uttermost parts of the earth. A number of us had been invited to go along to the special opening occasion. I was very much looking forward to being there and being able to see the new centre.

One of my close friends, Ann, a neighbour who lived a few doors up the road from me with her husband, Andrew, and three children, was also looking forward to the occasion. I had hoped we would go along together. Therefore, I was surprised when she asked me, "Do you think you could babysit for me so that Andrew and I can go together?" Ouch! I was planning to leave my husband John to look after our four children at home so that I could go anyway, but........? That would be quite a sacrifice. "I'll pray about it," I responded.

I had an internal struggle to be willing to give up going myself, but said to the Lord, "Ok, if it's what you want, then I'm willing, but I need a sign from you to confirm that it's YOUR will."

What was to be the sign? I knew that Ann's husband, Andrew, passed by our front gate on his way home from work at an approximate time each evening.

"Would you tell me, Lord, to go outside the front door at EXACTLY the moment Andrew is passing the gate if it is your will for me to babysit instead of going to the opening myself."

I then got out my iron and ironing board and got on with the ironing with an eye on the time. "Surely he must be here by now?" I thought. But with no inner prompting, I popped outside a couple of times to have a look to see if he was coming.

The time ticked by......the time had gone when

he would normally pass our house. It was looking hopeful that maybe it was not God's will after all, and I would be able to go myself. "Carry on ironing, Joyce," I said to myself. I waited with no more running outside to see if he was coming up the road.

The ironing almost finished, I suddenly heard the inner prompting, "Go outside NOW......." I placed the hot iron safely, and went to open the front door.

AT THAT EXACT MOMENT ANDREW WAS PASSING OUR GATE!!!!

I went down the front path and called to him, "Tell Ann I'll sit with the children so you can both go together to the opening of the OJ centre this evening."

It was clearly God's will, so my sacrifice became sweet, and I don't think I ever mentioned to anyone what it cost me to lay down my will to His greater will. It was a valuable lesson.......

DREAM ABOUT FAY'S FATHER

Many years ago I worked for a local estate agent in Leigh-on-Sea as a secretary. There were six of us girls who all worked together in one large office, and the sound of the clacking of typewriters equalled the pauses for clacking of voices as we caught up with each other's news.

We got to know each other well during the six years or so we worked together.

Several of us were married during that time, but one girl, Fay, lived at home with her parents with whom she was very close.

I eventually left to have my first baby, but we kept in touch for several years then gradually the busyness of life caused us to drift apart.

I had not thought about them for many years, when one night I dreamed clear as anything, that Fay's father had died. I awoke, thinking, "Oh, dear.........Fay will really miss her father. They were very close". I prayed for her and her mother that they would be comforted.

Later that week I read in the local paper the obituary for Fay's father.

I went round to her house with a card and put it through the letter box. Just as I was leaving through the gate, an upstairs window opened, and Fay's mother called me.

I was able to tell her "probably about the time your husband died, I was praying for you because I dreamed he had died".

I have never seen Fay since, and my recollection of her was that she was not someone who would have been open to talking about Jesus. However some years later I did by chance hear that she was attending a local church. God moves in mysterious ways!

GEORGE MUELLER STORY AND CASTLERIGG

Throughout my young adult life I had suffered years of intense pain from duodenal ulcers. These had led, on two occasions to severe haemorrhage and being rushed to hospital by ambulance with bells ringing.

On one occasion, in 1972, I was given several pints of blood by transfusion and I was too weak to set foot out of bed for three weeks.

The third time I haemorrhaged, there was an ambulance strike and they couldn't get me to hospital. I was ill in bed and instead of transfusion, I was given iron injections at home to make up for the blood loss.

We were booked to take the children to Castlerigg Camp in the Lake District again that year, leaving on a Saturday, but it seemed there was no way I would be well enough to travel. Just three days before, on the Wednesday, still too weak to get up, I read the following account of George Mueller by the captain of a ship he travelled on:-

"We had a man of God aboard, George Mueller, of Bristol. I had been on that bridge for twenty two hours and never left it. I was startled by a tap on my shoulder. It was George Mueller.

'Captain,' said he, 'I have come to tell you that I must be in Quebec on Saturday afternoon.' This was Wednesday.

'It is impossible,' I said. 'Mr. Mueller, do you know how dense this fog is?'

'No,' he replied, 'my eye is not on the density of the fog, but on the living God, who controls every circumstance of my life.'

He prayed a very simple childlike prayer.

"When he had finished, I was going to pray, but he put his hand on my shoulder and told me not to.

'First,' he said, 'you do not believe God will do it; and, second, I believe He has done it. And there is no need whatever for you to pray about it.'

'Get up, Captain and open the door, and you will find

the fog is gone.' I got up, and the fog was gone. On Saturday afternoon George Mueller was in Quebec."

Through this story, I sensed a kind of leaping inside. A sense that in spite of circumstances to the contrary, we would be at Castlerigg on the following Saturday.

We were......... It was as though resurrection life came into me and I was able get up from my bed to prepare everything necessary to get our family of six to the Lake District just three days later.......

COOKER FROM
BRITISH GAS

I desperately needed a new cooker. It was the time of free-standing cookers before fitted kitchens with built-in appliances began to come into vogue, and the one I had was really not very efficient. It cooked unevenly and burned things easily which should have been controlled by the thermostat.

I had researched them thoroughly, visited the gas showrooms in Southend and dithered over which one was best to buy. I had decided I wanted gas rather than electric, but the one I really liked with an eye level grill and a top which folded down was very expensive and I wasn't sure we could really afford it.

Finally, decision made, I set off to order the new cooker.

The traffic was very busy as I drove into Southend-on-Sea and I circled round several times, asking God to provide me with a parking space somewhere not too far from the gas showrooms. He didn't answer that one. Eventually I gave up trying to find somewhere to park and went home.

Meanwhile, my son Jonathan had gone to visit his school friend Robert, and while he was there, told the family about my quest to buy a new cooker.

When I got home from my aborted outing, Jonathan said, "Robert's dad works for the gas company. He said if you get in touch with him he can get you a discount on the cooker you want".

So I did and he did. So that was the reason I was prevented from finding a parking space – I would have missed the opportunity to have a considerable saving on my cooker.

So I learned that 'all things really do work together for good to those who love God and are called according to His purpose' even unanswered prayers....

RED ADAIR

At the end of April 1977 the story that most dominated the news was about a disastrous fire on an oil rig in the North Sea. This had been blowing for several days and was the worst of its kind worldwide at the time. It had spewed some 24,000 tons of crude oil into the North Sea.

All efforts at capping the fire had so far failed and the services of the world-renowned expert in the field of oil fires, Red Adair, had been called upon for his help. The weather had been very rough; the sea was raging with high winds at the time and it was difficult to get close enough to put out the fire.

I followed the story closely and felt really drawn to take this to the Lord in prayer because when Jesus was on earth he was in control of the weather and with just a word he calmed the sea of Galilee and stopped a storm; when the disciples were really frightened he just slept in the boat. And so I asked him if he would calm the storm in the North Sea so that Red Adair could cap the fire to put it out. I remember that I specifically used the words, "Lord would you please cause an icy calm on the North Sea!"

The next day I listened to the news with interest and the newsreader reported "there was an unprecedented icy calm in the North Sea today but unfortunately it was TOO CALM! What is actually needed is a wind of about 20 knots".

I came back to the Lord later that day, knelt by my bedside and said, "Lord I'm sorry, I got it wrong. What is needed is a wind of about 20 knots in the North Sea so could you please do that so that the fire can be safely capped? Thank you Lord".

Again the following day I listened eagerly for the news. The broadcaster reported "conditions were perfect today for the capping of the fire on the oil rig in the North Sea. There was a wind of about 20 knots which was ideal"!

Red Adair was able to do his dangerous work perfectly and the fire was safely extinguished that day. Jesus is the same yesterday today and forever!

I think I have only ever shared this story maybe a couple of times and one of them was with friends Margaret and Michael, neighbours of ours in Thrapston some thirty years later. Margaret is southern Irish and Michael is a big ex US Army Major. I felt led to tell this story to Michael. Red Adair was just a name I had heard on the news I had no idea where he came from, but Michael knew of his fame and I discovered recently that Red was from Texas, USA and so was our friend Michael........

WHEN GOD SAID 'NO'………A 'MOVING' STORY

Finding God's will for our lives is a lifetime learning curve. Through all my stories of God's presence in my life I have learned something of the will and character and love of God. Something of the gold to be found in the river.

Our semi-detached, end terrace house in Leigh-on-Sea, had been an exciting adventure when we moved into it when I was expecting my first baby. John's Grandma Emberson came with us because we had bought the house she previously lived in from her Landlord, a little two up two down terrace house with no bathroom and only an outside toilet. On learning that I was pregnant with my first baby we looked for somewhere bigger. In the new one there was plenty of room for the three of us, my husband John, Grandma and me – plus bump, soon to be our daughter Pauline.

Grandma had the back bedroom upstairs, and the back living room downstairs, and John and I had the two front rooms with the box room for the new baby. And we had a bathroom with a separate toilet! Luxury!!

Nineteen months later we were joined by new son, David, so we managed to squeeze him into the box room with Pauline.

By the time he had learned to walk, we learned that I was once again pregnant, and I think Grandma thought, "enough is enough" because she went along to apply for a new council flat in a block which was being built up the road.

This proved to be very timely as just five weeks before my due date, we discovered that baby number three proved to be not one, but two babies and twins Andrew and Jonathan joined the family just one week later after being diagnosed by (horrors!) X-ray – medical knowledge in 1965 did not extend to knowing the dangers of radiation to unborn babies.

We now had the whole of our little house so could spread. This was great. As they grew, the three boys shared one bedroom and Pauline still occupied the box room.

By the time the four children reached early teens, our little house seemed to have shrunk in size and we became somewhat desperate to move somewhere bigger.

My prayers became desperate, first of all to find a buyer because there were so many little three-bedroom semis on the market so that two years later we still hadn't found a buyer.

Eventually, after two prospective purchasers had backed out, we found one who really wanted the house and we looked around for potential homes.

There was a four bedroom chalet bungalow in Dundonald Drive that we liked, but it was really way above our price bracket.

Another that seemed ideal size-wise was in a different part of the town, and although it needed a lot of work doing to it, moving there seemed quite an exciting project. It had a very large garden, very overgrown with lots of trees and bushes. A lot of work to do, but hey! We were still young and it would be great for the kids and it was within our price bracket.

I spent a lot of time really pleading with God for that house! I persisted in prayer, believing it would become ours. At that time a lot of people were getting into contract races, but the owner assured us that the house would be ours. Then horror of horrors, he said his nephew also wanted the house, so he said it was first to the post – whoever was first to sign a contract could have it.

More pleading with God and chivvying up our solicitor who did a really good job to ensure we would be first past the post. We signed the contract and I went gleefully along to tell the owner.

I still remember the feeling I had as I stood at the door and told him we'd signed the contract. As I stood there I knew absolutely in my spirit that this was not the right house for us! Unbelievably, and to my great relief, he told me that his nephew was only one day behind us, so he was going to let him have it.

In spite of my urgent prayers, I had really wanted to be sure we were in the will of God, and had asked Him if this house was not His will for us, in spite of our pleadings, to close the door on it. Which He did, firmly.........

So now we had a buyer and nowhere to go.

We went back to have another look at the other house we'd liked, a chalet bungalow with four large bedrooms in Dundonald Drive.

Wonder of wonders, the owner had reduced the price such that we could now afford to buy it, which we did.

Why did God close the door on the other house?

Only in hindsight did I see the reason.

Twenty one months after our move, my husband John collapsed and died suddenly from a heart attack at the age of forty five leaving me with four teenagers. I was so grateful not to have been left in a house which needed a lot of renovation, plus a large garden which would have been unmanageable.

I was so glad that God in his wisdom, said 'no'.........

SUSPENSION OF TIME ON THE M6

We were on our way north by car for a couple of weeks holiday, the first week in the Lake District. It was a long journey from Southend-on-Sea to Castlerigg Camp near Keswick but the journey was worth it. The year was 1979 and we had been each year for the past ten years except one and looked forward to it. There had been quite a lot of rain that summer, but the sky was blue and the sun was shining as we travelled up the A1 which seemed to be the best option from the south. However, the traffic became increasingly problematic so we decided to go across country through the Yorkshire Dales to avoid the increasing traffic jam.

I was driving; it was my first long drive since passing my driving test, and John, my husband, let me drive. When we got almost to the M6 across the other side of the Yorkshire Dales we made a brief stop to stretch our legs and have a quick bite to eat of the sandwiches we had brought with us, mindful of the fact that we had tents to erect when we eventually arrived at our destination.

We were concerned because son David had gone ahead with a friend and her two small children and they would be anxious about our late arrival. No mobile phones then. Looking at my watch as we got back in the car, I prayed silently. "Please God could you cause time to stand still, so we can get there quickly, like you did for Joshua in the Bible when the Sun stood still for a day?"

I have no explanation for what happened next - I can only describe what I experienced. Our fourteen-year-old twin sons, Andrew and Jonathan were in the back of the car and my husband John was sitting beside me in the passenger seat as we reached the M6 a few minutes later. All I know is that at that point I was driving along in the outside, fast lane, of the M6 and although my speedometer did not register exceptionally fast speed we were passing a lot of lorries and cars on the inside lanes. I was aware that John appeared to be asleep and motionless sitting bolt upright and it was like being suspended in time. I remember thinking "maybe he's unconscious" - I spoke to him…….he didn't respond. I thought maybe he would slump over if he was unconscious and then on to me whilst driving which could be dangerous. I spoke to Andrew and Jonathan and asked them to see if their dad was sleeping or what was happening, but there was no response from them either.

I felt a little as though I was watching a film, and even though I was completely alert, had a sense of unreality.......

As far as I could see behind me through the driving mirror, the boys appeared to be either asleep or unconscious, they and John all sitting bolt upright. I had still the sensation of being suspended in time. That's the only way I could describe it.

I felt I was in an unusual state and which I can only now remember as an awareness of the presence of God.

We carried on northwards up the M6 and then turned onto the A66 at Penrith towards Keswick.

At that point John and the twins 'woke up' spontaneously all at the same time and just appeared to be completely normal. When I glanced at my watch, I realised that only ten minutes had elapsed since I looked at the time when we stopped before reaching the M6. I realised that during the drive up the M6, incredulously, no time had passed.

I have many times since studied the map and realised there was no logical explanation for what had happened but I still remember the experience very clearly. All I know is that God is outside of time – we are just moving through it - and I don't understand how but I know he can suspend time because he is Lord of time.........

BUNGAY

I was forty years old when I was widowed in 1979 with four teenagers to look after. It was a bitter-sweet time with bouts of overwhelming grief, but also a very special indescribable awareness of the presence of God which began at the time of the suspension of time on the M6. I knew what the Bible meant where it says that God cares for the widowed and fatherless.

However, six months later, I needed just to go away for a few days for a retreat and to deal with the grief inside me. Pauline came with me and we went to stay at Salem Christian Retreat Centre near Bungay in Suffolk.

It was March and bitterly cold when I donned my warm woollen coat and went out alone to trudge round the field next door to cry out all my pent up grief. I felt as though the Spirit of God was very close to me, and there were so many verses of Scripture just coming into my mind like the direct voice of God.

"I am your good shepherd…….even though you are walking through the valley of the shadow of death, it will not overwhelm you."

"I will never leave you or forsake you."

"Give your grief to me, for it is too great for you to carry alone – I am the man of sorrows, acquainted with grief."

"Come to me, take my yoke upon you and I will share this heavy burden."

Although it felt like words being spoken directly to me at the time, mostly I can't remember the specifics, but just still remember the sensation of comfort in great and intense weeping and grieving.

The Retreat House had been started by three lovely ladies, Lydia, Jean and Rosemary. I spent a while with Lydia because I wanted to talk with her about an experience I had had just before John died. She is I think the only person until now that I have shared it with.

For two or three nights with John in bed beside me, I had woken to hear gentle whispers, soft voices in the night, but not clearly enough to distinguish what they were saying.

The last occasion I was aware of it I actually

heard a voice say, "She's not ready yet."

"What was I not ready for?" I wondered.

For a month or so before John died, ever since the experience of the suspension of time on the M6 motorway, I had had a very close awareness of the presence of God. I was aware that the camp that year was to be the last for us together as a family. When we went on to Castle Howard in Yorkshire afterwards, camping with our first tent, I took a photo of John and as the camera snapped, I had the thought, "That's how I want to remember him when he's gone." I still have that photo in a frame.

So I kind of knew without knowing, and although doctors had said his chest pain was nothing to worry about, I think that I was being prepared for the ultimate separation.

It had come suddenly one Friday morning. I woke to find John in bed beside me groaning with pain. He didn't want me to call an ambulance, but I did. I also phoned the minister of my church, who arrived before the ambulance.

I told Lydia all the events as they had happened but especially my puzzlement about the voices.

"Well they were angels, my dear, preparing you for what was to come!"

How good of Him to be watching over us!!

After many years of prayer for his salvation, John had on one occasion asked Jesus to be his Lord and Saviour, but then some years had passed without appearing to move on with that commitment.

I knew that the Bible said 'call upon the name of the Lord and you will be saved' so as John lay dying, I asked him to call on the name of Jesus.......which he did ....loudly. At the hospital he was dead on arrival but they resuscitated him and he continued to call loudly on the name of Jesus, "please help me, please save me......" For years afterwards whenever I visited the hospital I could still hear that plea echoing down the hospital corridors.

Lydia prayed with me, and I knew a greater sense of peace.....

CAR MIRACLE

T here was an older, lady friend of Lydia's staying in the guest house near Bungay at the time we were there. She was just getting over an operation for cancer. She needed to get home to Norwich, so Lydia asked me if we could take her to catch the Norwich bus in Bungay.

We gladly agreed and she, Pauline and I got into our metallic bronze Ford Cortina. It had been John's pride and joy. We had bought it as an MOT failure for £400 and John took it to his place of work, where after he finished each evening, he worked on it to get it up and running. I had just recently passed my driving test and once it got through its MOT I was allowed to drive it.

There was however, something of a problem with it because frequently it would overheat, and spew out all the coolant water. I used to phone John to come out to me with fresh water to add after it cooled down. There seemed no way to re-solve this problem which went on for months. By the time of our visit to Salem, I was used to carry-ing water for the radiator for the unpredictable emergencies. In addition to the radiator problem, there was no heating in the car either.

We arrived at the bus stop in Bungay and sat in the car and waited….. and waited…… and waited……..no bus, and in the cold car, we were frozen.

"Not to worry," I said. "We'll take you home to Norwich."

The journey was uneventful and I was glad that the car was behaving itself.

When we arrived at our passenger's flat, we had a cup of tea at her invitation so that we could get warm, then set off back the way we had come.

Part way back, the needle on the temperature gauge started to go up until it was in the red zone and the water was thrown out of the radiator. I stopped the car in a gateway to a field to wait for the engine to cool before putting the emergency water in the radiator. But…….it was too cold to sit there for long, so I filled it anyway.

Off we went again. Back on the road towards Bungay.

"Oh no!" I said to Pauline. "The needle's creeping up to the red again. It's no good, we'll have to stop and call the breakdown people. I've no more water."

I had noticed we had just passed a telephone box (no mobile phones in those days!) so I drew to the centre line in the road and indicated to do a right turn so that we could turn round to go back to the phone box.

I can't adequately describe what happened next. An instantaneous and spontaneous surge of faith rose inside me, as I said to Pauline, "No, I'm not going to go back."

I cancelled the indicator, and continued driving. "I'm going to trust God to put this right," and to Him, I said, "Please would you clear whatever is causing the blockage and put this right," or words to that effect.

As I carried on driving along the road, the needle which had been on the red zone, slowly came back down to normal AND THE HEATING CAME ON WHICH HAD NEVER WORKED BEFORE.......!!!!!

I can still hear my daughter Pauline's incredulous voice..... "He did it......HE DID IT.....HE REALLY DID IT!!!!"

He really had and I never again had a problem with the car radiator overheating and the heating continued to work properly. While my husband was alive he looked after the mechanics of the car maintenance, but now I felt that God so many times resolved problems for me.

I used to say "The Lord is my mechanic" because many times I knew interventions and car miracles with that and later cars.

ISLE OF WIGHT

The summer after John died, I decided to take my four children away on holiday. They all pleaded for us to go abroad somewhere, but I'm afraid I chickened out of that as I'd never been out of the country. The thought of flying or crossing the stretch of water between England and France terrified me.

We settled instead for the Isle of Wight.....well, at least it was crossing the Solent on a ship and that was a bit of an adventure in itself!

We had booked into a holiday apartment near Ventnor. Arriving on a Saturday, I wondered where I'd find a church to attend on Sunday morning. On the way into the town I spotted a little building lower than the road down a steep embankment. That was where I'd go. Little did I know that that decision would begin to move my life in a different direction forever.......

There was a visiting speaker that morning whom I shall call Bill (not his real name) and he lit up the room. There was something about his bearing and preaching that made me want to ask questions about how I could move forward in my spiritual life. However, there were so many people around him clamouring to speak to him afterwards that I gave up. After all I was only a visitor......

When I had driven into the church car park, it was very hot, so I had chosen to go right to the far side and park in the shade of a tree.

After I left the building I got into the car and sat there asking God that if I was to speak to that man he would come and find me. There was one other car parked next to mine and I was aware of someone approaching it. It was the visiting speaker.

I don't remember much of the conversation I had with him, but it was on the lines of wanting to find some kindred spirits who were opening their lives to the moving of God's spirit. I was hungry to learn more.

"Come to the park this evening where several of us will be gathering, and I'll introduce you to a few people," said Bill.

With my four teenage children, we all went along to the park that evening and were introduced to Dick and Jo and their family who were approximately the same ages as mine.

Dick and Jo took us under their wings and we were welcomed into their home.

The following year they were going to a Bible conference, camping in Sussex. They invited us to join them. The main speaker was Terry Virgo, a man of God, who was teaching truths from the Bible which to a large extent were being recovered by the 20th century church. I was longing to be meeting with people who wanted to be led by the spirit of God.

I remember him saying, "God knows your heart. Just tell him and he'll show you what to do and where to go".

Which He did and suffice it to say that this led me to go to the fellowship where I met Bob who became my second husband. But that's another story.......

We kept in touch for years with our friends from the Isle of Wight until each of them died, first Dick, then Jo.

RIVER OF THE SPIRIT

The place I was led was to a few people originally meeting in the home of Chris and Margaret Chilvers but now moved into the local community hall.

This was very refreshing because we had left behind the trappings of traditional church worship and were learning to follow the Master, Jesus, together in the simplicity of his teachings.

I met and married Bob, and we stayed with those people throughout the 1980s. Bob had become a Christian from a totally unchurched and unreligious background, so he had no 'unlearning' to do. We learnt the simplicity of real worship, wonderful new songs that took us into the presence of God. So much we learnt.

I will share next some of the experiences we

had during our time with 'the Fellowship'.

When Bob and I met, we seemed to be often together in the same group, so no-one specially noticed our friendship developing. Eventually, towards the end of 1982, we each went to our home group leaders, who were elders in the church and asked them to pray about the rightness of marriage for us. They both were overjoyed and excited about the prospect and were very much for us! To me it felt very strange after having been a wife and mother of teenagers for years, to suddenly be a 'girlfriend' and fiancée again!

We planned our wedding for three months later......

FINDING ALAN

Bob and I were planning our wedding and sending out invitations. When I met him, he and his mother had lost touch with all their relatives, so mainly the worldly things he had to share with me apart from his mother, was a travel hair dryer and a potato peeler!! Plus a vast collection of American stamps and a number of chess trophies. We still have and are using the hair dryer, but the potato peeler has long since been lost and the stamp collection which had been kept for thirty years in two large boxes in the bottom of the wardrobe were sold at a specialist stamp auction. However, what Bob brought to me in terms of himself and his abilities was and still is pure gold.

His former life and former pals had been left behind when he became a Christian a year before, but there was one friend, a chess buddy named

Alan who Bob really wanted to invite to the wedding. We went along to his last known address ..... to no avail. He'd moved on.

We prayed about this. If Alan was to be found to invite, God would need to make a connection somehow......

We waited to see how He would do it............

One morning, as was usual, I set out to take our dog, Penny for a walk and used this time to take a wedding invitation to deliver to a friend.

Almost all the roads in Leigh-on-Sea either run parallel to the sea, or south to north away from it. Our chalet bungalow was the first house at the sea (south) end of our road, and a friend to be invited lived about five or so roads along parallel to our road, but at the far opposite northern end. This meant that the roads formed a rectangle. I could either turn right out of our gate, go down the length of our road, left along the main road to her road, or turn left out of our place, right along the shopping area and turn right again and walk down the length of her road to the bottom.

As I was leaving our gate, my first instinct was to turn right and go down the road, but I had a prompting as I did so that I should turn left and go the top end way round past the shops and down her road. Eventually I arrived at her house, put the invitation through the door and turned back up the road the way I had come.

Part way up the road, I saw a piece of paper on the ground – it must have been there on the way down but I had not noticed it – it looked like some kind of fairly important official document, so for some reason I picked it up….. not accustomed to picking up pieces of paper in the street.

One of those spine tingling moments as I read the information on it…..for it had the name and address of Bob's friend, Alan!!!

That evening, we drove round to see him at the address on the paper. Alan was amazed because he had no idea how the paper had been in the street where I found it, he had no connection with any-one in that street!

We told him "Alan, we have been praying to find you and I think God wants you to come to our wedding". He did.

I think we only saw him about twice after that, one occasion was when we were with our church in Southend High Street worshipping God in the open air with a gospel outreach. I had my eyes closed, arms raised and someone tapped me on the shoulder……Alan! I again reminded him that

God loved him and was seeking him.

I think he moved out of the area, but Bob and I prayed for him and had to leave him in God's hands and believed that God had a purpose in allowing us to meet up with him. In 2015, some 30 years later, when Bob had his 80th birthday party, I tried to find Alan on the internet and wrote to him inviting him to the party, but the letter was returned "unknown at this address."

WET SUMMER

One summer in the mid 1980's it rained ....and rained.......and rained.......throughout the UK. Everyone we knew had wet and soggy holidays. It seemed to be that England was just saturated in rain.

Bob and I went away on holiday with our touring caravan to Cornwall. Each morning with the rain bucketing down outside we would sit in the warmth of the caravan and commit our day to God. Bob was a very new Christian and although his life was given 100% to following Jesus he needed to see that Jesus was still able to do miracles today such that he did that are recorded in the Bible. Jesus calmed a storm on Galilee so I believed it was no problem for him to control the weather in UK.

We would pray and ask that God would lead us to go each day to where it would not be raining;

either He would lead us to the place where it was not raining or that it would not rain when we got to where we decided to go for that day. We would declare Jesus' lordship not only over our lives but also over the weather. We declared that it would be sunny wherever we went and although sitting at breakfast at eight or nine in the morning it looked like the rain had set in for the day still we declared that by 11 o'clock it would stop raining.

Wherever we went each day it was sunny and bright although the day had not started off in a very promising way.

How did we know that this was just happening to us? One morning, we decided that was the day to go and visit my mother's cousin on his farm just outside the town of Looe in Cornwall. We set off from our camp site in driving rain and as we got closer to the farm the sun came out, sky cleared to bright blue and the air smelled fresh and sweet.

We arrived to find Jack covered in dust struggling to cope with the hay harvest. Primarily, he kept deer for the local restaurants' venison supply but he took a few minutes out to show us his deer and also his man-made trout lake. He also told us that this was the first day it had stopped raining sufficiently to get in the hay harvest and had telephoned his friend, an accountant in Brentwood, Essex requesting his two teenage children, who had been on standby waiting for the weather to change, to come down and help him.

We sat on the paved patio outside the old stone farmhouse in the sunshine surrounded by sub tropical plants and enjoyed afternoon tea prepared by Jack's wife, Kath, a lovely hospitable lady. While we were there the two young people, a brother and sister arrived. They had come down by train from Essex to help Jack to get in his harvest. We asked them what the weather was like as they travelled right across England from Essex to Cornwall. They said that it had rained continuously all the way through their train journey but only cleared and became sunny when they reached the farm. This confirmed what I suspected, that God had answered our prayer for that local area.

On our return home when asked about our holiday we told the stories of how good weather had been with us every day on our holiday and that God had blessed us. Mostly people just responded by saying, "We'll come on holiday with you next year!!"

In years previously, before I married Bob, I had had a number of experiences of 'weather' prayers. After John died, I had bought a trailer tent so that I could take the family on camping holidays in comparative luxury.

As it is important that tents are folded away dry in order to stop the canvas rotting and being ruined either they need to be taken down in dry weather or spread out immediately you arrive home to dry before being folded away. However it's not so easy with a trailer tent. Although there was room to park the trailer at the front of our house, there was no room to open it up, so it was vital to have dry weather at the end of camping.

I would always pray for good weather and no rain so that the canvas was not wet. The prayers were always answered and during the four years I owned that trailer tent, I never had a problem. I remember on one occasion we were camping somewhere near Bude in Cornwall and looking up at the sky while we were putting all our pots and pans away, seeing a ring of dark clouds circling around where we were but only blue sky immediately overhead.

When Bob and I were married, he had never camped in his life - he much preferred hotels, but I suggested he tried the trailer out. He did once, but it just was not his 'cup of tea'. So we compromised and bought a caravan instead the following year and spent some thirty years caravanning.

MAN WITH MOHICAN HAIRCUT

Ever since my new birth as a child of God, I had believed the Bible and tried to listen to His voice and follow His leading and quiet promptings in my spirit. I made mistakes, and sometimes 'fluffed it'.

One of those occasions which I've deeply regretted ever since, was in prayer being given an address in Southend where I would meet a man with a Mohican haircut. I duly went along with my long suffering husband not knowing where the address was.

After we parked the car we discovered that where previously a house with that address once stood was now the site of Southend bus station.

As I stood there pondering, lo and behold, I turned my head to see on the corner was a young man with a Mohican haircut with his girlfriend just as I had envisaged!

I stood there silently, thinking 'Wow! ....but I don't know what to say....' Feelings of panic came over me.... so I said nothing and they walked away.

I told the Lord how sorry I was and to this day still remember that feeling of failure. All I could do was say, "I'm really sorry Lord, I messed up. If there's something you want to do in his life, please send someone else. Chase after him."

I've often wondered how this story would have continued if I'd been brave enough to follow through.

STORM
PROTECTION

The morning of 16th October, 1987 I woke to an almighty crash that sounded something like an express train thundering through the house.

Bob was already up, getting ready to leave for work by six a.m. .There had been gale force winds with increasing velocity all night reaching hurricane force by morning.

The sound of an express train was caused by a 10ft chimney stack on the roof of our house crashing down through the conservatory and leaving a huge hole in the roof. Andrew had been sleeping through it until the chimney came down missing him by about two feet.

We all shot downstairs. Bob had been about to let our dog, Penny, out into the garden through the conservatory just at that point. If he'd done so seconds earlier they'd have been killed, buried under a heap of rubble in what remained of the conservatory.

We lived in a chalet bungalow, with just two of the bedrooms upstairs set back into the roof space area, hence the reason the chimney stack fell lengthways next to Andrew asleep in bed. It doesn't bear dwelling on what could have happened to us that morning, but thankfully we were all safe.

Bob was still planning to leave for work at any moment, but the radio was on. A voice was giving the news of overnight devastation over the whole of southern England.

"Do not go outside, it's too dangerous," said the news reader.

Bob was going to take no notice. He had a job to get to. I had to persuade him to see sense.

In fact, the devastation outside was so great he would not have been able to go anywhere. When daylight came and the winds calmed, we were able to look outside. There was a huge tree lying along the pavement outside our house, and others multiplied all the way down the street.

When we managed to look outside into our small back garden, every tree and shrub was lying on its side, including a big old conifer I loved. Together with the rubble which used to be a chimney stack, the scene looked like something from World War 2.

Rain was still pouring through the huge gaping hole in the roof into our kitchen.

Later that day we managed to phone a builder friend who came and covered the hole with a tarpaulin but it stayed like that for three weeks because builders were so busy we just had to wait and take our turn for repair.

Tens of thousands of trees had come down that night in the Southend area alone, and an estimated 2 million across the whole of southern England and parts of Europe.

In the roads that ran parallel to the sea, all the trees fell across the roads, so they were completely blocked. In roads similar to ours running from north to south, they fell along the streets.

We had no autumn that year. Such trees as remained had lost every leaf.

When we ventured further afield, we saw that many houses had suffered greater damage than we had, especially those facing the seafront areas. Whole rows of houses had windows that had been blown in. In some cases we saw sides of buildings demolished and all the contents exposed to view. Fences were down everywhere.

We had come out of it comparatively lightly.

When we gathered that Sunday for our regular church service, everyone we met was praising God that not one of them had suffered any damage to their property........only Bob and Joyce!!!!

Why was this so? I don't know. Why were they all protected and we suffered quite severe damage? I don't know the answer to that, but I do know that our lives were spared because a few seconds and a few inches and there might have been a very different story..........

This reminded me somewhat of the story of Job, where he suffered much greater loss than we had. Though he slay me, yet will I trust Him.

We HAD been protected.

CLAIRE AND ST. MICHAEL'S CHURCH

Even if I've committed my time and steps to the Lord, when I have a nudge from him to do something I'm always a little surprised and say, "Is that really you Lord or is it me?" Sometimes it is best just to go with it and see if it proves to be the right thing to do.

On a particular Sunday evening I had that gentle nudge to go along to St. Michael's Church, just round the corner from where we lived, which I had never visited before or since. "Ok Lord, I'll follow that through".

"I think God wants us to go along to St. Michael's this evening, I don't know why......," I said to my long-suffering husband.

"Ok, then let's go," said Bob.

So off we went. We are not Anglicans, and bearing in mind this was not our usual church, we arrived wondering what this was about.

"Where do you want us to sit, Lord?" I asked silently in my spirit as we entered the church.

He directed me to a certain seat next to a girl all dressed in black from head to foot, and with blond hair covering most of her face so it could not be seen. "What do I have in common with this girl?" I thought, "and how do I begin to make a conversation with her?". These were my thoughts as the service got under way. We were not accustomed to a liturgical service, but managed to find our way through it.

At the end, I turned to the girl in black beside me and asked the only question I could think of, "Do you usually come to this church?"

"No," she replied. "I've never been here before. I've just moved here from Wales. Do you usually come here?"

"No," I replied. "I've never been here before either. Do you know anyone in the area?"

"No I don't, but back home I was given the address and phone number of someone who lives in Beach Avenue to get in touch with but I've lost the piece of paper it was written on".

"Well the only people I know who live in Beach Avenue are Jenny and Norman. They live at number 25."

"Yes I think that's the name", said the girl who introduced herself as Claire.

This obviously must have been the reason we were directed to visit that church on that particular evening......to connect a lonely girl in a strange place to some potential friends. She told me she was a drama student enrolled at the drama school just along the road.

Someone came up and spoke to us at that point, then Claire left the church just ahead of us. As she reached the gate, I again had that inner prompting, "Invite her back home for a coffee." Slight panic on my part as again feeling what would we have in common to talk about, but as Christians we belong to the one family of God, so I braved it and called to her, "Would you like to come back to our house for coffee?"

"Oh, I would, thank you," she responded.

That was the start of a friendship which continued during her time in Leigh-on-Sea at the drama school and I think more than once we drove her to Wales and met her mother.

On one occasion I remember, we were going

with her to a conference in Cardiff but first we went to her mother's home. They lived in Bridgend which was beyond Cardiff, but her mother had prepared a meal for us before we went to the conference. The family had previously lived in Hong Kong, so the meal we were given was a Chinese dish and we were presented with chopsticks to eat it with! Quite a feat to try and eat quickly, and I think we were a little late for the meeting!

Back to the first occasion when we met Claire, she asked if she could bring a friend round to see us, which I think was the next day. Thus we met Valerie, a lovely little country girl from Dorset with long glossy black hair, also enrolled at the drama school and they both started dropping in regularly and I think we became a little home from home for them. Then Valerie's sister, Dawn, moved up from Dorset to be with her and to start nursing training, so she also started 'dropping in'. They rarely ever all came at they same time, but as one of them left, another would arrive, almost daily.

Then, at a neighbour's house, we met Kizzy, another girl who dropped in frequently and for whom we provided a base for friendship and sharing. At that time together with my own family, our lives were enriched and fulfilled by these young people who all attended at times the same church fellowship we did. Although this happened more than 30 years ago, I am still in touch with them via Facebook.

And all of this came about because one Sunday evening we obeyed a prompting from God to go 'outside the box' and follow his leading.

SCOTLAND, PAULINE AND 'GO' TEAM

When Bob and I announced that we were planning to tow our ageing Sprite Musketeer caravan up to Scotland in June 1987, daughter Pauline decided to come with us as she had one week's holiday coinciding with our two weeks, and would return from Inverness by coach.

We towed northwards, a long trek all the way to Alastair's Hill Farm near Invergarry. Remote and beautiful, each caravan was pitched on an individual area away from others. That far north it was barely dark at midnight in midsummer and we enjoyed the long bright evenings to walk and talk and take photographs of the idyllic scenery.

As was our usual routine even when we were on holiday, we looked for a local church to attend on Sunday but had difficulty finding one. I commented, "I think there needs to be some church planting up here!"

Pauline responded with, "If God wants to plant a church up here He can send me!"

In the church we were part of in Southend-on-Sea, belonging to a group of new churches, much church planting was taking place often involving several individuals or families moving to a new area and forming a new church.

We put her on the bus for the long journey back to Essex, but clearly she would have liked to stay longer in that wonderful setting.

Later that summer, we again towed our caravan to Wales for a church convention at Builth Wells.

Pauline was with us, and some of the other young people who dropped into our home regularly. Pauline had recently found a rented flat to make her home, and was about to get a cat on her return home and settle down.

The leaders of the churches represented were calling for young people to give a year of their lives to work for God in a church in one of several locations around the country. They would have to live by faith which meant about £3000 would need to be funded from their own resources or supportive family and friends. A number of young people responded, then my own daughter came to me and said "Mum, I think God wants me to go on a GO team". (GO stood for Gospel Outreach).

We certainly didn't have that kind of money and neither did Pauline. I gulped as I responded, "Well if God is calling you, then somehow He will provide".

To this day I've never known how all that money came in, and for our part, we were certainly stretched in our faith, but every penny she needed was provided.

September came and off she went to Solihull, one of the locations the church leaders decided needed a team to be sent. We had no idea what Solihull was like and only knew it was somewhere near Birmingham. So we took her up to Solihull from Essex with some trepidation, a little apprehensive as to what awaited....but if that was where she was called by God to go, then that was ok!!

......We were pleasantly surprised to say the least by the big expensive and opulent houses in the tree lined roads of Solihull. A very affluent area.......

She was housed with some other girls in a rented house, and some young men in the team in another. Always quite a shy and quiet girl in public, that year gave her confidence and brought her out of herself as she and the other team members went into schools and on the streets telling people of the love of God.

The following year, in June, all the GO teams from wherever they had been sent, were called together to go to Inverness in the north of Scotland for two months to help with a new church plant!!!

I remembered her words a year earlier "If God wants to plant a church up here, he can send me"! That could not have been engineered by man, only our amazing God could do something like that......!!!!

The bonus to this story was that in Solihull she met Desmond, who later became her husband, and she never returned to live in Essex. They still live and work in Solihull.

THE WHITE CAR

B ob and I needed a new car to replace our existing one which was becoming unreliable.

Our church was going through a phase of 'naming and claiming' which involved being specific and telling God exactly what you wanted. We did.

"Lord, we need a car, please, one not more than five years old, white, with four doors. We only have £1000. We'd like to hear about it through a friend and please could we have it in the first week of July."

We left it with our God and waited to see what would happen.

One day while out shopping, we decided to pop in on our friends, Joyce and Eric. A young couple were also visiting them while we were there.

Conversation turned to their need to sell their

car.

"How much do you want for it?" I asked.

"£1000" they said.

Was this 'our' car............?

"What colour is it and how many doors does it have?"

"It's white, with four doors," they responded.

"And how old is it?"

"It's five years old, but we can't part with it till the first week in July."

Spine tingling, we knew this was the answer to our prayer.

We bought the car..........it was the worst car we had ever had. Mechanically we had problem after problem with it.

Yes, God had answered our very specific prayer, but we forgot to ask for a good reliable car. From this we learned that according to Psalm 106 verse15 He (God) *gave them their request, but sent leanness into their soul.*

No more naming and claiming, His will is best and that is what we need to seek not what we want or think is best.

A painful, puzzling, but useful lesson.......

VISIT TO ESSEX WATER COMPANY

[2] "Go down to the potter's house, and there I will give you my message." [3] So I went down to the potter's house, and I saw him working at the wheel. [4] But the pot he was shaping from the clay was marred in his hands; so the potter formed it into another pot, shaping it as seemed best to him.

[5] Then the word of the Lord came to me. [6] He said, "Can I not do with you, Israel, as this potter does?" declares the Lord. "Like clay in the hand of the potter, so are you in my hand, Israel.

Jeremiah 18:2-6 New International Version (NIV)

◆ ◆ ◆

It would seem that when Jeremiah went down to the potter's house he knew that God was going to speak to him there. I have had a few of these experiences in my life. One such was during our time of seeking his will regarding our time at Southend Christian Fellowship.

During that summer Bob and I frequently took out for trips our three mothers (how was that, you may wonder!). It was his mother, my mother and my first husband's mother. We decided to visit the Essex Water Company's open day.

As we set out I had a very strong sense that I would hear from God that afternoon regarding the church we were in. And so it proved.

We were wandering around their trout fisheries, looking at round pools of fast moving water, each with different sizes of trout within them.

The water was being moved rapidly in a circular motion because trout like to be swimming against the current. As I stood and watched, the water was being driven in a clockwise direction which caused the fish to swim against the current in an anti-clockwise direction. To the onlooker, however, as we gazed with interest, the fish appeared to be stationary. They were swimming with all their might, but were going nowhere!

As I watched, the word came to me, "That is what the church is like, there's a lot of activity, trying very hard to swim against the current of the world's way of doing things, but you're going nowhere."

"Lord, please show us what you want us to do, because we need to break free of the endless cycle of 'doing' and move forward into what You want us to do and be."

As we made our way home that evening I was deep in thought and sensing that I had heard from God.

As years had gone by, the gathered group grew and grew till we reached nearly 300. That meant organisation. And teams. Teams to clean the building, teams to serve tea and coffee, teams to sell books, teams to set up the PA, etc. etc.

During the summer of 1989, we had met up with a few people, again in their home, who were moving into the realm of the simplicity of worship and finding the presence of God. Refreshing. I was hungry to maintain this simplicity in our lives.

In the big group, we had moved into larger and larger rented premises, with the ultimate goal of owning our own building.

The one we were led to buy was a dilapidated cinema in the east end of the town. Bob and I spent many hours painting and decorating to get the place in a temporarily usable state.

By the end of the '80s, we were longing for the simplicity of the early days. We were up to our eyes in activity.

I had said to someone in the summer, "I believe God will show us by the end of the year what we have to do."

I had been trying to find the heart of God and hear His voice. Worship times in our new building had become so loud that I couldn't hear His voice there at all. In addition a project I had started and run for six years, I had attempted to lay down and hand on to others, but was met with rejection. "What will you do instead?" I was asked. I didn't know but responded that I would like to find out. I felt that I was 'in a box'.

At home one day, I heard Him speak. "I want you to be a tent people. To pull up your tent pegs and move on wherever I lead you." But I had a husband who seemed quite content with all the activity.

On the last day of 1989, Bob had set off for the meeting at 8.30 that Sunday morning to open the building and get the PA set up. He was then on the welcome team to greet people at the doors.

Because most of the other members of the group were younger with young families, we had also had to clean the building before we started. Afterwards, I was in charge of the bookstall which I had started and now occupying a separate room, overseeing my team there, and we were also taking our turn on the refreshments rota serving teas and coffees. Phew!

By the time we had finally cleared up, seen everyone had left the building and as last out locked up by 1.30, we were exhausted. But had we met with God? No.

As Bob locked the doors that New Years Eve, I knew it would be our last time there. We were exhausted. "Do you think we could go somewhere else next week?" I asked my husband.

"God hasn't told me to," he replied.

"Have you asked him about it?" I queried.

We had family round for lunch, so when we had eaten, we sat in the lounge to relax. It was a while before I realised that Bob hadn't been seen for a while.

Eventually he reappeared from the bedroom. "Where have you been?" I asked.

"Praying," he said.

"What about?"

"Our future."

I pressed for more information. "And what did He say?"

"He said we're to be a tent people and move on!" I had not told Bob that was what I had heard because I wanted him to seek and hear for himself.

That confirmed that we were to lay down our tasks for the Fellowship group and find his will for our lives......another bend in the river. What lay ahead round the bend........?

BOB'S OPERATION

When we left Southend Christian Fellowshjp on New Year's Eve, 1989, we felt a little like Abraham when he left Ur of the Chaldees not knowing where he was going!

We had gone to the leadership and told them about our leading. Mostly they graciously said, "If that's what God is saying to you then we release you and you must go, but we shall miss you and if it doesn't work out, please come back".

So we left knowing we had their blessing.

We joined with the small house group we had been meeting with over the summer – it was a resting place, but we knew it was only to be temporary. We stayed with them for fifteen months, during which, together with Peter and Sheridan and Chas and Debbie, we were led into setting up a new chapter of the Full Gospel Businessmen's Fellowship International (FGBMFI). This was very strange because Bob and I were not business people. But this is very much an evangelistic organisation reaching out to businessmen with the gospel and Bob and I booked restaurant venues and speakers and did some of the admin. Peter was the Chairman. During that time we had some amazing contacts and saw God speaking and reaching people with His truth.

Again we knew this was only for a season, and it was also a training ground for what was to come.

Shortly after that Bob had to go through a very serious operation when it was discovered that he had cerebrospinal-spinal fluid leaking from around his brain. It took two years to find out how it was happening and even an MRI scan did not help to make a correct diagnosis. We had also gone to a London hospital for him to be investigated by several eminent medics from all over Europe to see if they could work out why cerebrospinal fluid was leaking out through his nose. MRI was still in its infancy in England when Bob was sent to St. Marylebone Crypt which housed I think one of the first MRI scanners in England.

When it was arranged to operate at the Throat Nose and Ear Hospital in Gray's Inn Road in London by eminent neuro-otologist Mr. Gerald

Brookes, the scan pictures were misinterpreted and what they thought they were seeing was a tumour growing up from his only ear into his brain. Bob was born with only one ear, the left side was just a malformation with no eardrum. The operation on the right was his only hearing side, and we were warned that the operation could leave him totally deaf, with no means of hearing whatsoever.

Bob and I prayed a lot about the future, and wondered if we should learn sign language to help us communicate after the operation. But we were at peace and decided to leave the matter of his hearing in God's hands.

The day of the operation arrived and I think I went to work just to take my mind off what was happening in London – with instruction to phone at a certain time when i would be able to drive to London to see him.

In due course, I set off with my friend Margaret whose own husband had had a brain tumour affecting his ear and causing deafness some 20 years previously.

I drove as fast as I could from Leigh-on-Sea up the A13 to the east end of London with Margaret beside me, not knowing what we would find when we arrived.

We walked into the ward and found that Bob

had had half his hair shaved off, and his head was swathed in thick padding and bandaged. I spoke to him, and in spite of all the dressings, he could hear me!

I was flooded with such a sense of relief and thankfulness.

It transpired that what they had thought they were seeing on the scans, a tumour going from the ear into the brain, was in fact the brain which had prolapsed down through a gap in the bone of the skull, and was mangled into the inner ear! It had taken several hours and intense skill on the part of Mr. Brookes, who had never seen a case quite like it, involving not only extricating the brain tissue and lifting it back up to where it belonged, but also removing bone from his thigh to repair the gap in the skull.

We had many years of follow up visits to London for regular checks and in fact he still needs regular local checks almost thirty years later.

PULLING UP
TENT PEGS

As a result of the events in the previous chapter, when Bob was offered early retirement soon after his return to work after his op, we decided he should take it, as getting to work for six thirty on cold winter mornings was taking its toll.

The tent pegs had been pulled up, but I think we were still packing up the tent which was quite cumbersome.

We needed clear guidance for the future. We had visited a few churches nearby, but nothing that we clearly felt we were being led to. We had visited Leigh Road Baptist Church, a good, sound traditional evangelical church, that had recently appointed a new minister, Roger Martin and we had gone along to listen to him once.

That spring, for the first time ever, we decided to go to Spring Harvest, an event which took place in several holiday camp locations around the UK over Easter. We booked into the one at Minehead in Somerset.

We were still very much asking God to show us what was our next step church-wise.

I was increasingly picturing Roger Martin's face when asking God about his choice of church for us.

One day while strolling around the Butlins camp site, I asked Bob, "When you're thinking about a church, does anything come to your mind?".

"Yes," he replied. "I keep picturing Roger Martin's face".

Wow!! Was this clear guidance?. Believing very strongly that any guidance should be confirmed by three witnesses, we waited.

Shortly afterwards, we walked into one of the cafes, and who should be sitting there, but .....yes....Roger Martin! We had not known he was at Minehead.

Next thing that happened, while going to one of the seminars, on the stairs we met Ian Coffey whom I'd known many years before at spirit led meetings in Great Wakering, Essex.

He greeted us and asked about what church we were attending.

"We've left Southend Christian Fellowship." I answered.

"Yes I know, I'd heard that."

"Well we're praying and asking God where he wants us to go next."

"Have you considered Leigh Road Baptist Church?" asked Ian. "My friend Roger Martin is looking for people like you to go and join him to bring some changes there". Wow again!!! This would appear to be confirmation.

And so that turned out to be our spiritual home for the next four years.

WHERE NEXT?

In 1990 Bob and I knew we were in a time of change. I don't know how to describe it, it was just a 'knowing in the knower'. Or perhaps it could be described as a sensing in the spirit; a kind of intuition.......

We booked a camp site at Danbury in Essex for a few days away in our caravan with the object of 'getting away from it all' and just seeking guidance from God about our future. We really wanted to know His will, not just our own ideas. We had 'tried a few doors' but these had all remained closed.

The end of 1989 had seen communism falling in Eastern Europe and a Revolution in Romania which ousted the evil dictator Ceausescu and his wife. My sister Pat with her husband Derek had volunteered to work on a two week mission with YWAM. Although this stood for Youth With A Mission, they were also sending older people on short term ventures. They were asked to go and work in a Romanian orphanage.

They returned full of stories of the need there, and the dreadful conditions in the country following the revolution. The country had been brought to extreme poverty while Ceausescu used the natural riches of the land to build himself a huge palace, the second largest administrative building in the world, at the expense of the Romanian people.

Many people could not afford to feed their children and so they were abandoned into orphanages where they might receive some meagre subsistence to keep them alive.

On their return, Pat and Derek told stories of the appalling conditions. "It's like England after the War, similar to when we were children".

My immediate thought was, "I don't think I'd like to go there!"

Many years previously, I had heard a Romanian Lutheran pastor, Richard Wurmbrand, speaking at a meeting near my home in Leigh-on-Sea. He had spent a total of fourteen years in a Romanian prison, mostly in solitary confinement, while there was extreme persecution of Christians by the communist regime. The conditions he had to endure were horrendous but one thing I have always remembered him saying was, "While the

Christians were being persecuted and tortured, they prayed for you in the West."

How amazing! I later read and still have a copy of his book 'Tortured for Christ'.

I now believe that it was as a result of those amazing prayers that so many, possibly thousands of people, responded to the need when the borders opened and 'the west' could go in to help.

I had watched with amazement the scenes live on television as the revolution took place in Romania – never dreaming that we would ever go there and even meet many people with first hand stories of that event. Some two thousand people lost their lives on the streets at that time, over a four day period just before Christmas 1989.

On their return, Pat and Derek invited a family to come to England for Christmas 1990. Bob and I thought that would be a good thing to do and asked them to arrange for someone to visit us at Easter 1991.

They chose Luminita and Mihail Teodorescu, a couple who were both disabled, Luminita from childhood polio and Mihail with encephalitis. We sent a letter of invitation and they duly arrived at Heathrow Airport, looking very Eastern European with their solemn grey clothing and black felt hats.

Luminita and Mihail told us that they worked

part time for the Romanian Evangelical Society in Bucharest which income supplemented their small pensions. This Society had re-formed since the revolution having originally been set up in 1920 by Duminitru Cornilescu, the translator of the Bible into the modern Romanian language. They had brought with them a letter from the Society by way of introduction and validation.

On their return home, the president of the society, Daniel Cuculea, wrote to us inviting us to partner with them to help them from England with the work they were doing.

Was this God's voice to us? It certainly was not what we would have chosen to do. Besides which, it would involve setting up a charity but we had no idea how to do that – it was way beyond our experience or capabilities.

We put the letter on hold because we were about to go off on holiday to a Bible camp near Malvern. We took the letter with us intending to spend some time in prayer.

Soon after we arrived and set up the caravan, we made a cup of tea then we got out the letter and re-read it. "No that's just not possible," we decided. "We've no idea how to do that." But we asked that if this was God's will for us, he would confirm it by providing the help we needed.

Then we got on with completing the jobs to

make the caravan secure. We had just bought a new hitch lock for the caravan, and in order to fit it over the tow bar, we needed to release the cap. We just couldn't work out how to do it.

"Let's ask Roland," I suggested. So we went across to another caravanning friend a few pitches away and asked him for his help. Simple when you know how....it was done in a jiffy.

We stood chatting, then found ourselves telling him about the letter we had just received and the request to set up a charity to help them.

"Do you know how to do that?" asked Roland.

"No, we don't. It's way beyond our experience."

"Well I do," he said. "Setting up charities is part of my job. I can help you with that"!

Eventually, he did the following year and became one of our first Trustees.

During the week we were away at Malvern camp there were a number of other confirmations we were on the right track. In addition to those, I was petrified of flying and though I had nervously flown a couple of times, I had been suffering from severe panic attacks in enclosed spaces. We had driven to Italy to visit a friend in 1989 and every time I came to a tunnel through the mountains, of which there were many, I would suffer pains in my chest and my legs would go weak. Ever since

I could not go into lifts or other enclosed spaces and as to flying.....that was definitely a no no.......!

I had been healed much earlier from lifetime problems of this nature, but it had returned due to stress.

At that camp in Malvern I attended a seminar one morning, during which there were several 'words of knowledge' for people, one of which was for those suffering from claustrophobia. That was me, so I asked for prayer, during which I was told that it was related to birth trauma, particularly because I was a breach baby. This made sense as with breach babies the head comes out last instead of first and therefore can leave a sense of being trapped leading to claustrophobia. After laying on of hands and prayer, I knew I was healed. I have met a number of people since who suffer in this way and I usually ask if they knew if they had been born breach and often the answer would be in the affirmative.

Therefore, we were able to fly out to Romania in October 1991 to meet the members of the Society and to learn more about what they were asking of us.

When we arrived we were met by Luminita and Mihail and introduced to two brothers Daniel and Teo Cuculea, Aurel Coste and Titi Manolache. We had lengthy discussions with them to find out in what ways we could help them, and learned of their plans to continue the work of Cornilescu by translating and printing books. We could also help them with their humanitarian work.

THE ADVENTURE
BEGINS.....

T he following year, 1992, we bought an old Luton van for £500. Everyone we contacted was wanting to help the humanitarian aid effort to Romania. Therefore, when we asked a vehicle hire company for help they gladly lent us, free of charge, a long wheel base transit van.

There was a team of six of us planning the first driving trip: Bob and I, my son David, Chris and Charlie from the church we attended and our friend Mary.

The house was filled for weeks as people brought to us, clothing, food, printing paper and ink and other essentials to help in those early days. We filled the two vans. Every box had to have the weight listed and lists made of the contents not only in English, but also in Hungarian and Romanian. Bob was especially good at this work and even managed to find someone who knew Hungarian for the translation.

The "Sally" shipping line kindly gave us free ferry crossings from Ramsgate to Dunkirk for the two vehicles and large "SALLY" posters in red to stick on our vehicles for ease of identification. Little did we know how useful they would be as we set out on our adventure......

The first problem we encountered was with the hire van. When we attempted to start it to drive off the ferry at Dunkirk it simply refused to fire and we had to be pushed off the ferry!

After a jump start we set off on our journey across Europe, which took five days instead of the anticipated three, one because our aged Luton van could not be persuaded to travel above fifty miles an hour and two we lost a day because I had to spend a day in a German hospital with intense pain which they diagnosed as 'intercostal neuralgia' or shingles in English. The pain was not helped by the fact we couldn't find a bed for the night and had to spend it parked in a lay-by, sitting upright. Most uncomfortable.

The two vehicles managed to stay in convoy all the way through Belgium, Germany, Austria, and Hungary. This was necessary because whenever we stopped the vehicles, we had to use jump leads to restart the transit van.

My sister and her husband had advised us, "Whatever you do don't drive after dark in Romania because it's dangerous, you don't know what you might come across".

However, one member of our team overruled this advice and because it was still daylight, thought we should keep going and cross the border into Romania in early evening.

What we encountered were potholes such as I'd never seen in my life, needing considerable skill to navigate. We rounded one corner after dark to find a flock of sheep being herded through the middle of the road, and further along a horse being given water from a bucket also in the middle of the road! Old men were sitting smoking outside little houses, waving cheerfully as we went past. There were very few vehicles on the roads then.

We trundled along through the night, managing to stay together until........we reached Sibiu. Mostly the towns had two routes. You could either go straight through, or follow a sign that said 'lorry route'. We had stopped for a snack and changed team members. Bob and I had been travelling with Mary, and David with Chris and Charlie. Mary and David changed over so David was with us and Mary in the other vehicle. Charlie set off ahead of us and by the time we followed a few seconds later, he was nowhere in sight. Which way had he gone? Had he chosen the lorry route, or gone straight through the town? Quandary.......

We chose to go through the town with little traffic at that time of night.

We seemed a very long time catching up with them, so when we reached the far side of the town, we thought they must have gone by the other route and must be behind us. We stopped the van, but kept the engine running because they had the jump leads and we would not be able to restart without them.

We waited for some time, but they didn't come along. Were they behind us or in front? We picked up some speed knowing our vehicle, the transit, could travel faster than the Luton. Still no sign of them. After some miles we stopped for a break to again wait to see if they caught up. This time we waited on a hill slope, and stopped the engine knowing we could start by running down the hill.

Eventually, we decided to just keep going through the night the rest of the way to Bucharest some sixteen hours drive from the border in those days and in those conditions. We had no idea if they were in front or behind us. The problem was, they didn't know the address we were heading for, and I was carrying the team's money! Bear in mind this was before the age of mobile phones, so we had no means of communication. It was an adventure!

We could only pray.

At one stage, as light was beginning to creep up in the early morning, not daring to stop on a level road through a beautiful mountain pass with a steep cliff on my right and a drop to a river on my left, I fell asleep at the wheel. Bob and David were asleep beside me. I woke after what was probably only a few seconds by the sound of rubble under the wheels. I had run off the road onto a stretch of gravel which woke me up.

Only about another hundred miles or so to Bucharest......

We kept going and eventually found our way to Titi's house. I don't remember how as there was no SAT NAV in those days. I think I may have found a telephone kiosk, phoned them and they came out to meet us.

We told them the tale of our missing friends in the other vehicle. I was just thankful that Mary was in the other vehicle, because she was very level headed and had been to Romania before. I knew she would not panic and was a lady of great faith.

We were plied with food. "You must eat, and then you will sleep," we were told.

I tried to resist sleeping and felt we needed to go out and try to find our friends, but they insisted we had to sleep while Titi and Aurel went out to look for the others. All they knew was that the vehicle they were looking for had a large sign with "SALLY" on it.

They went out to the main road into Bucharest and at that exact moment, trundling along the road came 'Sally'. Titi and Aurel ran out into the road arms waving to stop them.

Afterwards, we were told that when two strange men had jumped out into the road in front of the Luton they were quite frightened, because there had been an incident with someone trying to stop them on the way, but this time the linkup was made and the team was back together.

Coincidence or God's timing? I think the latter.

ROMANIA, THE CONTINUING STORY

For the next fifteen years, we were in and out of Romania once or twice each year; in the early days, sometimes driving and sometimes flying. The rest of the year we were in constant contact, fund raising, sending needed materials and personnel. We acquired a second-hand fax machine – oh the wonders of the then modern technology when we no longer had to rely on snail mail, but a letter sent by fax could be reproduced instantly at the other end of a phone line. However, due to poor phone connections in Romania, the letters more often than not had elongated words looking as though some mischievous imp had set fire to the ink and it had melted and run down the page!!!

I always knew when it was time to go again because I would have a certain dream, either we were flying or driving and I would know that indicated the way we were to travel.

We had some amazing adventures and the charity we set up came with us through three different house moves and church moves and wherever we were, people got behind what we were doing.

When we were working with the Romanian Evangelical Society in Bucharest, at one time we were donated about twenty desktop computers by Customs and Excise in Southend when they were updating their computer system. Our friend Bob who worked for them and had been with us on one visit to Romania, was instrumental in arranging this.

From another source we were given printing ink, boxes and boxes of paper, and a printing machine from a Christian printing house in Sussex. Once we were given a photocopier, and managed to arrange for that to go out by road with another group.

There seemed to be a vast network of organisations working in Romania so we would often manage to find someone who would carry some large item for us. Anything taken into the country could only be donated to hospitals, orphanages or charities. We took the photocopier we were given to a group who were storing relief items in a warehouse in the Midlands, so we were able for a small donation to ask them to carry it for us. This had to be taken to a hospital, I think it was in Brasov, several hours drive from Bucharest and from there our friends were able to collect it.

I remember they drove to fetch it through four feet of snow in Titi's aged home made jeep.

In 1992, I had a small legacy from an aunt and put the money towards our first and only ever brand-new car. It had to have a Diesel engine because there was no unleaded fuel available in Romania at that time. I had frequent battles with lady fuel attendants who tried to insist on putting petrol in my car...no self service then. Motorina (diesel) was for lorries not for the masina (car)!! We were able to choose the registration number from a selection and chose one with the letters DAR because I knew it to be the Romanian word for gift. It was our gift from God.

When we got to Romania that year we found that the Society had recently acquired two cars for their work. Both had the same registration letters......DAR!!!!

When we were driving through Romania we were usually given addresses where we could stay. There is nothing like Romanian hospitality and several times we stayed with Gheorghe who was caretaker of a church in Rimnicu Valcea. He spoke no English, but managed to communicate with us that if ever we were in any trouble anywhere in Romania, he would come to us. This proved very timely on one occasion.

In 1993 we were driving through the country with Mary and stopped in a lay-by next to a river to have some sandwiches. A man was showing some unwanted interest in us and came to the van shouting in Romanian. He seemed quite threatening. We closed up the rear double doors quickly and jumped in the van. (By then we had our own long wheel based transit which was reliable). It was Mary's turn to drive.

"Quick, get in the van and just DRIVE!" Which she did with the poor man hanging on to the vehicle's running board. Eventually he let go and we got away. However, in panic mode, Mary had forgotten to release the hand brake.

We had travelled several miles before she realised, by which time the brakes were thoroughly bound and overheated. Now what were we to do? No breakdown service in that country. You were reliant on friends. Then we realised where we were – just passing Rimnicu Valcea where lived Gheorghe who had said to call him if ever we were in any trouble. We managed to drive into the town and find him. He sorted out the problem for us and wanted us to stay for the night, but we had to be on our way.

◆ ◆ ◆

Our involvement with the Society in Bucharest eventually wound down by 1999.....they were self sufficient and by now had established a printing house and were able to print and publish Christian books, magazines as well as some secular material. Meanwhile we had moved to Thrapston, near Kettering in Northamptonshire and Graham Timson, the minister of the Baptist church we atended, on learning of our connection with Romania, asked us to find a small work the church could support.

We drove out in 2000, Bob and I with one other man, Dave from the church, having emailed ahead to tell our Romanian contacts of our plans. By now we were into the technological age and communication was much better.

When we got there we were plied with requests for help with a number of projects, some twenty in all ranging from a block of half-built apartments to building a church in Galati, up near the Danube Delta where a man with a face like an angel was hosting so many people for christian meetings in his home that some people had to be asked to stay away so that we could visit. The service went on for several hours, all in Romanian, and I managed to keep awake in the warm atmosphere by taking video of the occasion.

Most of the projects were way too big for our little church back home and after almost two weeks, we hadn't found anything suitable.

On the last day before returning home we met a 21-year-old young man, Cristi Golas, who was buying bread and making sandwiches from his own pocket daily to feed some street kids. Some of these were older young people who had grown up on the street.

We were privileged to go along with him to meet some of them. When we told Graham about this, we all agreed this was a project we could run with. For the next six years we supported Cristi and his team of workers and renamed our Charity 'Seeds of Hope for Romania'. We took teams of people out from England to take some of the street kids away to a camp in the mountains. This involved de-lousing and having hair washed with nit shampoo and bathing in the river. We then provided them with clean clothes and so they were ready for camp. A doctor then had to examine them to pass them as clean and fit enough for the camp. One team from England would go for the preparation and another would join us for the actual camp. We had some adventures there, too many to recite here.

Our friend Laurentiu from Constanta on the Black Sea coast told us about the girl he had met through family and friends and excitedly told us about his impending marriage in 1999 to Ema from Rimnicu Valcea. She came from the church where we had visited Gheorghe who helped with the repair of our van in an earlier story.. We invited them to come and stay with us in England for their honeymooon. Laurentiu and Ema made their home in Constanta. In July 2000, their first baby, a son called Filip was born. Then on Bob's birthday 16th December 2001, we got a phone call from them to give us the news that Naomi was born.

Three hundred or so miles away in Pitesti, Cristi Golas, by now married to Cami, was also expecting a baby. We got a second phone call that there had been another birth that day, Bianca had also arrived on 16th December 2001.

Two baby girls both born on the same day on Bob's birthday three hundred miles apart!!

There was no connection between the two families and we didn't expect them to ever meet. However, in 2012 on our last trip to Romania and the first which was just a holiday to visit friends, we went to Bucharest to stay with Laurentiu and Ema in their home in Bucharest..

There were people we wanted to visit in Pitesti,

so Ema drove us the 80 or so miles from Bucharest. We visited Cristi and Cami and the two little girls, Bianca and Naomi, who shared a birthday with Bob, met for the first time.

I was able to take a photo of them together and asked the two mothers what time each was born.....it was just one hour and 300 miles apart!!

LIDIA AND MARIA
AND OTHER
STORIES

On one of our visits to Romania we were taking Christian books in the Romanian language for distribution to prisons and churches and individuals who might need reading material but not able to buy it. When we first went to the country in 1991, it seemed that there were very few Christian books available in print. The only one we knew of was John Bunyan's 'Pilgrims Progress'. During the communist regime Christian books were forbidden and we were shown on one occasion where a family's collection of books was kept – buried in a hole in the back garden in a metal box close by the wooden shack which housed the hole in the ground toilet. So any books were very precious and closely guarded – on pain of imprisonment if discovered.

We were taken to visit Lidia and Maria in their tiny home which had been built some years previously by family members. The one room they lived in was about 10 feet long by about 6 to 8 feet wide and the walls were covered by the usual Romanian woven carpet-type hangings. There was just one bed in the room which these two ladies, a mother and daughter shared and the cooking was done in a tiny lobby by the entrance door. This was their only living area and the toilet facilities were just the wooden shed outside covering the toilet pit.

We had first met Lidia and Maria on a previous visit but they had no telephone and no means of communication and they did not speak any English so on the day that we decided to visit them they had no means of knowing that we were going.

They greeted us with great excitement and Lydia declared, "I dreamed last night that you were going to come today and that you would bring us books.....!!!"

The warmth of their welcome and their kind hospitality matched the warmth of the heat in their tiny room. They plied us with cake and mint tea. Usually the mint tea was made from mint grown in the garden.

On another occasion I had been told of the problem of someone with a sewing machine that had a part missing but our friend was unable to translate into English the name of it. I was able to produce from my bag a couple of bobbins that for some unknown reason I had popped into my bag before we left England. These were just what Mariana needed for her sewing machine so she was soon up and sewing again.

This was in a village where there were just dirt roads some 10 to 15 km from Pitesti. Three brothers and their wives lived alongside each other and had built their own houses. In order to build the houses, they had first of all to make the bricks, one by one, in a mould, then bake them in a kiln until they had stored enough to start building.

Mariana's sister, Fivi, had been working in the garden with her vegetables and her thumb had become badly infected and was looking very inflamed. She clearly needed antibiotic to stop the infection spreading up her arm and into her blood stream.

I suggested she visit a doctor, but she couldn't afford it. Penicillin at that time was available over the counter, but the cost was prohibitive for many people. That day I suggested we tried dunking the thumb in hot water to try to draw the infection to a head. We went back to our friend Luminita's apartment in Pitesti where I had a supply of sterile dressings we always carried with us, and also my own supply of antibiotics which I always carried as I am allergic to penicillin and knew that was the only one available in Romania.

I took them back to Fivi with instructions to take them as directed and for three days went back and forth to the village to re-dress her thumb. I dread to think what may have happened to her without our intervention, but this was just another example of carrying suitable equipment when we had not known what needs we would meet with.

MORE GOD-INCIDENCES

The Department of Clinical Neurophysiology at Southend Hospital where I worked as a medical secretary was in dire straits. We were down to one EEG technician with a waiting list for EEGs of up to six months. The hospital tried unsuccessfully to recruit. EEG technicians were a rare breed. In addition, few people with the necessary training and qualifications wanted to come to Southend-on-Sea. It was 'the end of the line' and there were plenty more jobs in more desirable places. I was constantly having to apologise for the length of waiting times and juggling appointments to keep some spaces for urgent needs.

This needed some urgent prayer. "Please Lord, could you send someone to fill the vacancy? If there's no one who wants to come here from this country, then please send someone from another country…..?" And as an afterthought I added, "and if possible could you send a Christian?"

The prayer was answered shortly afterwards when Sarv, a trained EEG technician in Toronto, Canada, felt God led him to answer the advertisement and come to England with his Canadian wife Ann and three little girls. He had been looking on the Internet at job vacancies, together with a map of their location and felt the location of Southend 'jumped out'.

We welcomed them to our home on occasions as they welcomed us to theirs.

During conversation we discovered that he had a dad and sister in Birmingham.

"That's interesting," I said, "I've got a daughter in Birmingham." Then amended the statement because Birmingham is a huge city. "Actually my daughter lives in Solihull".

Sarv laughed. "My sister also lives in Solihull!"

"Well, to be more specific, my daughter lives in a

village which is part of Solihull called Dorridge".

Silently, he fetched an index card with an address on it and handed it to me.

It was the house next door to my daughter and son-in-law and Bob and I had already met his sister and brother-in-law, a very nice Sikh couple!! Coincidence or Godincidence?!

While they remained in England, we fellowshipped with them, sometimes having meals together. After some time, they quite suddenly left England to go back to Canada and we lost touch with them.

We often thought about the family but had no way to find out their address because we had had no opportunity to say goodbye. I asked God to somehow put us in touch with them.......then waited to see how He would do that........believing that according to the Bible there is nothing hidden that will not be revealed if we ask our God who knows all things.

A few weeks later, we went from Leigh-on-Sea where we lived to Southchurch the opposite end of the town of Southend to do some shopping at a new Lidl that had recently opened. We did the shopping, then, because it was a very hot day, we sat outside in the car eating an ice cream we had just bought.

In the car we were parked next to, a simple homemade cross dangled above the dashboard. "I wonder if the people who own that car are Christians?" I said to my husband Bob.

Just then, a young lad came out of the store pushing a laden shopping trolley, his parents and siblings in tow behind him.

I watched a trifle nervously as the boy carefully manoeuvred his way with the trolley between our two cars without damaging either of them.

They loaded the shopping into the car then I said to my husband, "Let's go and speak to them".

"I've seen the cross in your car, are you Christians?" I asked. "Yes, we are". They told us their names were Steve and Debbie and they were stocking up on shopping following a visit to Toronto, Canada.

In one of those strange moments when you're not quite sure why you say something, I asked, "Do you know Sarv and Ann (xxxxx)?"

"Yes, that's who we went to visit" they said. "They're friends of ours and we met them when they were working in England".

They had met because both families were home schoolers and in the course of that they met through a home schooling association.

And so we were once again able to be in touch with the Canadian family.

On one occasion we later went to stay with Steve and Debbie and remained in touch with them for several years. Whilst we were with them we were able to speak with our friends on the other side of the Atlantic. Also, for a while the three little Canadian daughters used to send us lovely handwritten letters with their family news.

TERRY WAITE

I was invited to go along to a Lydia Conference in Brentwood, Essex. I had never been to one of their intercessory meetings, before or since. There was a roomful of women, powerful intercessors and the atmosphere was electric when they prayed. They sought to find the mind of Christ and his leading before launching into prayer.

Terry Waite had been much in the news in 1991 about his imprisonment in Lebanon. Despite many attempts, the British government had failed to secure his release.

"Terry Waite was the Assistant for Anglican Communion Affairs for the then Archbishop of Canterbury, Robert Runcie, in the 1980s. As an envoy for the Church of England, he travelled to Lebanon to try to secure the release of four hostages, including the journalist John McCarthy. He was himself kidnapped and held captive from

1987 to 1991." (*Wikipedia*)

Someone in that room said, "I really believe we should pray for the release of Terry Waite".

The room resounded with the prayers of women, one by one, and then collectively, till a lone voice spoke out........

"I see a picture of a door opening....I think it means he's going to be released!!"

There was much praising and thanking God for the answer to their prayers.

A few days later it was announced in the news that Terry Waite was to be released!!!

GWEN

Our friend Gwen was a lady of great faith. She was my son-in-law Desmond's spiritual mother having led him to know Jesus when he first came to England from Kenya. They worked together at NatWest Bank.

As Gwen got older, by the late 1990s, much as she loved visiting people, she struggled to cope with stairs and carrying luggage. She particularly faced with some trepidation the prospect of having to carry her case up steep stairs when she arrived back at her home railway station after a holiday.

On one occasion, she told me that as she stood at the bottom of the flight of steps, she said a silent, "Please help me Lord"!

The next moment, a younger woman gently took the bag from her, saying, "I'll take that for you" – and strode up the stairs with it.

Gwen followed as fast as she could, but when she got to the top where her case stood, she looked around to thank her helper ....but she was nowhere to be seen!!!

Gwen said that it was not possible for someone to disappear from view so quickly, and came to the conclusion she must have been an angel!

DIANE

I worked with Diane for seven years, secretaries sitting at opposite desks in the reception area of the Department of Clinical Neurophysiology at Southend Hospital.

Diane and I had some similarities in common in our early lives, and sometimes we were able to discuss these, but she made it plain as soon as she found out that I was a Christian, that I was not to talk about my beliefs – that if she wanted to know anything, she would ask me........so I respected that.

Eventually she told me that she had been out to lunch with an old friend who had shared with her that she had been 'born again'.

""What does it mean to be born again?" asked Diane.

Remembering my promise not to talk about my beliefs, I was quite guarded ....but she had asked.

My answer was mumbled and very low key, afraid to offend.

Diane suffered from very severe and debilitating migraine attacks. These sometimes lasted for hours, or even two or three days involving absences from work.

One morning I arrived at work as usual. Diane and I switched on our computers and while waiting for mine to load, I stood by the radiator to get warm.

Diane told me she was getting a migraine.

"Do you believe if you pray for me, I will be healed?" she asked.

'Help Lord' ...... silent arrow prayer. 'What do I do?'

Panic started to rise inside me. I felt the response was, 'be honest'.

To my surprise, what came out of my mouth was, "No, I don't, but you do, so we'll ask".

The simplest prayer ever, eyes open standing by the radiator......."Please Lord, heal Diane's migraine".

Then we got on with our day's work.

Nothing more was ever mentioned about the

episode. I can't say Diane was healed. All I know was that as far as I remember she never again went off sick with a migraine.

ANOTHER 'MOVING' STORY

In 1998 I was approaching retirement age. I had enjoyed my work at Southend Hospital as a medical secretary, but was starting to wonder what lay ahead for us, Bob and I were praying about our future. We had for some time wanted to move out of Leigh-on-Sea to somewhere less busy. Years of driving to work through heavy traffic took its toll in terms of stress. We had friends living in Northamptonshire and very much liked the area and the wide open skies above the gently rolling countryside.

In March of that year we were on our way to visit Pauline and Des in Solihull. On the way, we met our friend Margaret who had suggested we had a look at the small town of Thrapston, where she had some friends. We met up with her friend Ken who showed us around Thrapston Lakes because having lived close to the sea for most of my life, felt I needed to live somewhere near water, either a river or lake. Thrapston had both.

Then we looked around to see what houses were available. We stood on the corner of Wainwright Avenue looking up the road to where there were two For Sale boards.

"Why don't you go and knock on the door and ask about them`' suggested Ken.

"I don't think I could do that", I responded, "besides they look much too grand and expensive for us".

So we continued on our journey to Solihull and left Ken a list of requirements which we felt would be needed in a potential new home.

Later that day the phone rang at our daughter's home. It was Ken! He had had the courage to knock on one of the doors and ask about the price of the house. The owner had shown him around and he reported that he was able to see the river in the distance from the back bedroom window! The owners had someone already interested in the property, but would let us view it on our return on Monday. The price, surprisingly was within our budget, because house prices in Essex where we lived were higher than further north,

So we viewed it on the way back.

As we entered the house, Bob and I both immediately felt a sense of "this is home". The owners had had a slightly lower offer than the asking price, so we said "if you will give us two weeks to sell our house, we will give you the full asking price".

So we went home and prayed, "God if it is your will for us to have that house, could our house be sold within two weeks to a cash purchaser and with no property to sell".

By the time we had instructed an estate agent, they had come to measure up our house and got it onto the market, ten days had gone by. Our house was advertised in the local papers coming out on the Thursday, just ten days from the time we had viewed the house in Thrapston.

On the Friday, while I was at work, I got a telephone call from an estate agent in Kettering to tell me that the house we had seen in Thrapston was sold.

Disappointment set in. How could this have happened? The owners had promised to give us two weeks to sell our house and the two weeks were not yet up. But my next thought was "if that's to be our house Lord, then it will still be our house. It's up to you Lord".

The next day, Saturday, we had three viewers lined up who had responded to the advertisement and made appointments with our agent.

The first people to arrive to view had asked the agent not to let anyone else view the house until they had seen it.

They fell in love with it. They had been waiting for a house in our area to come on the market.

"We'll give you full price for the house, it'll be cash and we don't have to sell our house first to buy it!"

Wow! Within two weeks we had our cash buyers. What to do now?

Bob and I prayed and drove up that afternoon to Thrapston and knocked on the door of 'our' house. No answer. The owners were out.

What should we do? We felt that the right thing to do was to remind them of their promise to give us two weeks to sell our house.

I wrote a note saying, *we have sold our house within the two weeks you promised to give us, to a cash purchaser who is able to proceed straight away,* and went back to the house to put it through the letter box.

By that time the owners had returned, so I handed it to them and repeated its message. They had no recollection of promising to give us two weeks to sell our house. They said that the other person who wanted the house worked for the estate agent in Kettering and they had had pressure put on them to agree the sale. However when we confirmed our offer of full price, they agreed to sell it to us.

We had no doubt that this was confirmation that it was to be our new home.

The river was to take another turn........

THE FATHER'S HEART

The next chapter was written more than 20 years ago in 1998 at the time it happened and is therefore written in the present tense. I had forgotten about it until finding it recently among some old documents on my computer

Andrew is in the Middle-East. He last telephoned me more than three weeks ago and we were cut off in the middle of the conversation.

He had given me a telephone number to ring back, but the number was unobtainable. We were in the middle of discussing what he was going to do and where he was going to go next, but before any conclusion had been reached, the line went dead.

He had mentioned that he wondered whether to go to Egypt, or to Romania, but I did not know what he decided.

On trying to get hold of the telephone number through directory enquiries, I found that there was nothing recorded for "Noa Hostel" in Tel Aviv, the address he had given me.

Panic set in.

My son is aimless and in a foreign country. He does not want to return to England. The source of his hurt and pain is here because the house of which he had been part owner was no longer his and he feels that he now has no roots.

The pain in my heart, not hearing from him, is great. I feel as though I am grieving inside. I feel a little as the Father must have felt in the Bible story of the Prodigal Son. How the Father's heart must have ached because the son had opted to leave the family home and go away and spend his inheritance.

I wonder if the younger son in the story had made a promise to keep in touch with his Father? Probably not – we don't know the circumstances of his leaving.

We had an arrangement with Andrew that I would telephone him at the last known number I had, but if he was going to move on somewhere else, he would contact me. However, his visa had expired in Israel, and he was planning to move on.

All my prayers to ask God to cause him to telephone home have so far not been answered.

Everything in me wants to go out and buy a

plane ticket to Israel and go and look for him. I just want to hear his voice and know that he is all right. To know where he is and that he still cares about me enough to telephone me.

How the father heart in the story of the prodigal son must have leapt when he saw his son in the distance, making his bedraggled way home again.

I felt a prompting from the Lord today to write this down. Then I picked up a book that I had borrowed yesterday from the Christian Book Service and read some words which encouraged me.

"Are you seeing it now? The whole time you have been bombarding heaven with prayers that seemed to go unanswered, I have been at work. All the while you were questioning, I was quietly healing, restoring, and rearranging.

"But you needn't feel guilty over the lashings about of your flesh and your mind that have occurred in this process. Even these have worked for your good; they have deepened your capacity to understand My heart and character.

"For instance, you have learned a vital lesson about My sovereignty. Now you are seeing that the phrase "the sovereignty of God" is not an escape clause nullifying My promises. My sovereignty is your stronghold of security! Not only do I fulfil my commitments, but I do exceedingly above and beyond all you ask or think or imagine.

"Yes, I do keep you guessing sometimes as to how I will answer your prayers – but that is because I AM a Person, not a principle to be manipulated. I AM faithful and reliable, but hardly predictable. Predictability is a characteristic of law and principle, not life and personality. Now you will sing "Great is Thy Faithfulness" and know what you are singing about!"

And the reading on the opposite page also spoke to me:

"Stop reasoning and ask! I have opened the windows of heaven and you need only to ask! Ask and ask largely, for I joy to shower abundance upon you, causing your joy to ignite the faith of your friends.

"I told you earlier of the harvest you would reap from those days of sowing in tears, did I not? Then ask. The harvest is ripe, and the day of your freedom has dawned! Stand in agreement with singleness of heart, children, for today is the day of My power. Rejoice and be glad in it!. I AM!"

A further week went by, and slowly I came to a place of peace. One of the things which I had found difficult to cope with was the fact that possibly Andrew might not have booked his plane ticket himself, and had I not done it for him, the outcome may have been different. His desperate cry from the heart "What else can I do, I have no home, nothing to keep me here!" tore at my heartstrings and vividly stayed in my memory.

I felt guilty and was grieving inside for my own part in the separation. Then the Lord reminded me that in the story of the prodigal son, the father had agreed to give the son his share of the inheritance, even though he knew that he would go and waste his living and end up living with the pigs. He had agreed to help him to go. And so I found peace that the Lord did not blame me for possibly getting it wrong, even though I had believed that God wanted him to go to Romania with us.

After four and a half weeks, and much prayer and a special time of prayer in the church that there should be contact with Andrew, Bob and I both felt that the unknowing was coming to an end. I had worked out in the logic of my mind that he must be in Egypt, as he had not drawn any money from the bank for more than a month, and that was the only place he could afford to live on the money he had with him. However, on that Monday morning we went into the bank and discovered that he had drawn some money from his account the previous day. (I had a joint bank account with him so that I could transfer money into it for him), During that evening, just after preparing dinner, I had a thought; I scarcely know how to describe it. A prompting in my spirit? Hardly a voice, but definitely a nudge from the Lord. "Ring the Red Sea Hostel in Eilat (Israel)." That was where he had spent some time previously.

I telephoned there, hardly daring to ask in case the answer was yet another negative.

"Do you happen to have Andy Fenton staying there?"

"He's not actually staying here, but he happens to be sitting in the lounge here at the moment."

Wow! "Bob, I've found him" I cried. In fact it clearly was not me, but the Lord. Praise Him.

We re-established contact, and discovered that he had been "miffed" that I had not telephoned him back, not realising that I did not have the correct telephone number.

Thankfully, the stress and strain of that time

was over. Little did I know the further stress which was to come just four days later involving other members of my family involving severe health problems.... But I'll save that story for another book!!

ANDREW IN ISTANBUL

In 1999 Andrew was staying at a hostel in Istanbul. We were visiting friends in Salem, Oregon, USA. Several phone calls with Andrew halfway across the world revealed he was in something of a dilemma because, through no fault of his own, the bank had changed some accounts over and he had no access to money.

What should he do?

I knew that Turkey, and Istanbul in particular, was not too far from Romania with only Bulgaria in between. We had friends in Romania, so I suggested that with the only money he had left, he buy a train ticket from Istanbul to Bucharest and I'd arrange for someone to meet him at Bucharest station.

I was concerned how he'd cope with that. "How

will you know I've got on the train?" he asked.

"I'll ring the hostel after the time you should have left and if you're not there I shall know you're on the train?" I suggested.

The next day at the appointed time, I duly rang the hostel in Istanbul. He answered the phone.

He was in panic mode. "Now you've phoned me I'm held up and I'll miss the train!"

"Just go, get a taxi to the station........"

Still in Salem, there were an anxious couple of days during which I telephoned friends in Romania to arrange to meet his train.

Would he cope, would he manage to catch the train in time? Without any contact, Bob and I could only pray.

The train journey across Bulgaria took 24 hours and I learned afterwards that he had nothing to eat or drink during that time.

Eventually, I made contact with our friends in Bucharest. He had arrived. Hungry, thirsty and dishevelled, but safe.

Thankfully, he had left Istanbul just before we heard on the news that there was a devastating earthquake. I also discovered that the hostel where he had been staying was severely damaged.

"Stay there and wait for us. When we get back from America, we'll come out to Romania and fetch you home." Which he did and we did.

Eventually we heard the story of that day. He had bought the ticket but missed the train and had to chase it up the line in a taxi to the next station.

However, we didn't learn the rest of the story until a few weeks later.

We were with Andrew in a shopping precinct in Kettering when a tall young man with afro hairdo came running up to us.

"Hi Andy, how are you doing? The last time I saw you, I was helping you get your ticket at Istanbul train station!"

I was so grateful to know that our prayers had been answered and Andrew had had help when he needed it......!

DARREN

My son David married Nancy in 1986 and they had two children, Christopher and Emma. However, before he met Nancy, David had had a relationship with a girl, who had given birth to a baby boy called Darren. However, she wanted the baby but not the relationship with David, so it entailed a lot of heartbreak because he was my first grandchild and I was not able to see him. Initially when he was about two weeks old the mother came round and placed him in my arms and said, "This is your grandson". But then her rejection of David made it very difficult to keep in touch, so eventually we lost touch.

David and his wife Nancy visited him for a while until he was about two, when his mother decided to stop any further contact.

The only time I saw him was once when Bob and I were walking along the beach at Leigh-on-Sea. A little fair-haired boy of maybe four or five leaned over the promenade wall, looked down onto the beach and said, "Hello……"

I said, "Hello" back, then looked across to where his mother was pushing a pram. I don't think she saw me, but when I realised who she was, I knew that I was speaking to my grandson and he did not know who I was. That was a painful moment.

Every year when his birthday came round, David and I would remember him and wonder what he was like.

When it got to his eighteenth birthday, David said to me, "If you want to look for Darren, I don't mind, but don't tell me you're doing it because I couldn't bear the rejection if he did not want to know me."

So unbeknown to David, Bob and I set off down to Southend for a few days to see if we could find him. We knew as he was now of an age to make his own decisions he could decide if he wanted to know us.

First of all, we went to look at the Electoral register in the Council Offices in Southend. I wrote down the addresses of everyone with the same surname as Darren. There were a number of them. We went to a church to see if we could find a friend of the family who might be able to put us in touch, but drew a blank there.

Bob and I sat in the car and prayed and asked

God to lead us to the right address.

The first two addresses we tried, we drew a blank, but at the third one, a lady opened it and when I asked, "Are you related to Darren (.....)" was told, "Yes. He's my great-grandson."

I told her that I was David, Darren's father's mother and asked her if she would get in touch with Darren to see if he wanted to meet us as he could now at 18, make that decision himself. I left her my mobile phone number and said he was to call me if he wanted to meet us while we were in the area, within the next couple of days. We then went to visit son Jonathan and his family.

We had only just arrived when my mobile phone rang. "Hi, this is Darren. I'd like to meet you. Mum says you can come round to our house." He gave me an address in Southend. He continued "I know about David, Pauline, Andrew and Jonathan, I have been looking on Genes Reunited on line."

My insides felt as though a lot of butterflies were going wild as Bob and I drove to the address Darren had given me. What was I going to find when the door opened?

The young man who invited us to go inside just looked so familiar, I felt as though I had always known him! We hugged each other and went inside. He told me that just the day before we were there, he also had gone up to look at the Council

Electoral Register to hopefully find his father but had drawn a blank. Obviously that was because David had moved out of the area.

He had also gone onto the Genes Reunited web site where a relative had posted our family details and amazingly just that very week sent an email to the family member to enquire if those names he found had ever lived in Southend.

So he assumed when we turned up on his great-grandmother's doorstep that it was a response to the email.

We then arranged for him to come up to Thrapston to meet David and his half brother and sister Christopher and Emma. His mother had also had another son whose name was also Christopher.

The rest of the story is too long to tell, but suffice it to say that Darren met his dad and the rest of their family and we have been in touch ever since and that is now some fifteen years..........

Darren and his fiancée Jemma have two children Khye and Mya and they are my great-grandchildren. There is going to be a wedding in the spring which we are looking forward to.......

BROTHER
YUN VISIT

I t was with some excitement that we learned
that Brother Yun, the author of 'The Heavenly
Man' was to be speaking at a church in Kettering, near to where we lived in Northamptonshire. Entry was by ticket only, which was free,
but tickets had to be limited as a high uptake was
expected.

Our friend Sylvia very much wanted to go and
hear him speak, as she had been on a mission to
China taking Bibles for the underground church.
Everyone looked forward with expectancy to the
stories of God moving in supernatural ways in
that country where believers were being persecuted by the communist authorities.

By the time Sylvia tried to get two tickets for
herself and her husband, there were none left and

there was a waiting list should any be returned.

Sylvia laid her disappointment before the Lord.

Bob and I went along to the meeting and found ourselves seats on the balcony where we had a good view, not only of the platform, but also of the lower floor of the church.

Knowing that Sylvia had been unable to get tickets, it was with great surprise that we spotted her and her husband Ron being ushered to seats near the front.

"How did that happen?" we wondered.

We learned afterwards that this humble man of God, Brother Yun and his small team, had needed to find somewhere to stay in Kettering. The host church which had invited him enquired of the local information office what accommodation was available in the town.

Sylvia and her husband ran a small B&B guest house and this was the one selected for Brother Yun to stay.

So not only did she meet the man himself and have him staying in her home, but they were special honoured guests when they were shown to VIP seats..........

PRAYER WALKING

Only one man turned up for house group that evening in early 2003, so the three of us, Dave, Bob and I decided we would go prayer walking round our housing estate in Thrapston.

This involved walking around together but instead of chatting to each other we'd 'chat' with God and ask him to show us how he wanted us to pray for the people in each of the houses.

We spoke softly whatever came into our minds to pray, some quite specific although we had no prior knowledge and only later found in several instances the prayers were 'spot on'.

In particular, a few doors up the road, we prayed for a particular family as we were passing their house.

"Please Lord, would you bring them all along to church on Sunday,". I've no idea why those words came out of my mouth.

The following Sunday, we gathered as usual at 10.30 for the start of the service. I looked around and noted a new family had arrived. It was the family from the house we had been passing when we prayed that they would come to church on Sunday.

They did, mother, father and the two children. They had never come before, and to my knowledge never came again.

I think we had some lessons to learn here about persistence in prayer, but failed to learn that lesson on that occasion... ......

AGREEING IN PRAYER

Throughout our married life, until recent years when Bob's Alzheimer's made it impossible for him to remember or understand any more, whenever there was a special offering at any meetings we attended, we would always separately ask for guidance as to how much we should give. When we both had a figure in mind, we would compare and discuss and invariably found we had been told the same amount. This was in addition to our regular giving to the church.

This principle of asking God how much He wanted us to give worked well, even when we were not together.

I remember on one occasion going along to a meeting and an offering plate was being passed round.

"How much do you want me to put in?" I arrowed up....

"Nothing," was the reply. "I don't want you to put anything in".

"But I've got £x in my purse," I said.

"Yes I know you have, but you're not to put anything in."

All this took place silently and only seconds passed. 'That must be my imagination' I thought. I'd better put something in.........

I looked in my bag to get out my purse. It wasn't there!!! I had left it at home.

I felt there was a silent chuckle from heaven........"told you.......!!"

YET ANOTHER 'MOVING' STORY!

W e lived in Thrapston for 15 years and much could be written about our time there, but suffice to say that during that time around 2007, Bob started to show signs of considerable memory problems and eventually was diagnosed with Alzheimer's Disease at Addenbrookes Hospital, Cambridge.

This was another "Ouch!" moment for me, grieving for what I was starting to lose in Bob as he became somewhat withdrawn. He attended Addenbrookes Hospital Memory Clinic a number of times at six monthly intervals before they finally confirmed the diagnosis and started to treat him.

Bob accepted it calmly, even humorously, as at each visit to the hospital he anticipated being asked the same routine questions and doing the same tests.

"What's the name of the current Prime Minister?" was the usual one. Then we had a change of Prime Minister to Gordon Brown. Bob couldn't remember his name. In the waiting room he asked me, "Quick, tell me the name of the Prime Minister, I can't remember it!" I didn't tell him as it would have defeated the object of the test.

However when he came out from the doctor's room, his face showed relief. "They didn't ask me the name of the Prime Minister, but wanted to know the name of the only female Prime Minister". He could remember that one!

As a result of Bob's steady, but slow decline, by 2012 I was thinking that we needed to start thinking about a future move to downsize and simplify our lives for the future. I was not sure what this would mean, but we prayed and waited for God to show us.

Out one day in nearby Raunds, where we had some business to attend to, we were just setting off back home towards Thrapston, when I had the thought "call to see Val and Alan" some friends we had met at Thrapston Baptist Church. I stopped the car and got out my mobile phone.

"Are you at home for a visit?" I asked them.

"Yes, it'll be great to see you, come on round",

said Val.

Always very hospitable, they invited us to stay for tea. During that time, they told us about some flats to rent in St. Ives, near Cambridge, where there was extra care available if needed. It sounded interesting but we may not have thought any more about it had we not been going to Addenbrookes Hospital the following Friday for an appointment. On the way back on the A14, we saw a sign for St. Ives and on the spur of the moment turned off into the town to see where the flats were located. The manager was not available at that time, but we made an appointment to return the following week to have a look around.

Our names were put on a list to await a vacancy.

We felt this was divine guidance so looked for a church in the area. We found "The Bridge" and as soon as we walked in, felt it was where we belonged. It reminded us of our earlier times at Southend Christian Fellowship where Bob and I had met and Bob just loved the worship. He had been in the worship team at Thrapston Baptist Church, but due to the decline in his mental capacity had had to give that up.

It was best part of a year before a flat became available but we were sure it was where we were meant to be, so waited patiently then downsized from our four bedroom house to a one bedroom flat!

We moved in June 2013..........another bend in the river.......!

We really needed a two bedroomed flat, but took the available one in order to make the move, being assured that if and when a two bed one came up we could always move again,

2015/2016 saw a block of new flats being built just five minutes walk from where we lived. Bob had started receiving care for help with showering and we were grateful that the carers were on the premises. We would regularly walk round to look at the new block of flats as they rose from the ground. A plan of the layout was attached to the workmen's gate to the building site and as we looked at it, we decided if we were able to move there, which one we would like. Ever since we had joined "The Bridge Church" they had been praying that eventually we would be able to have a two bedroomed flat.

Eventually, by the end of 2016, the care company based in our Anchor Housing block ended their contract and were given the contract for care at the new extra care flats. A friend from the church was invited to the opening ceremony at the new flats and he said to us, "See if you can get flat number 103! It's beautiful!" It had a different number to the numbering system on the building plan, but having been invited to a priority visit with a view to being accepted in the new block, we went along and asked to see flat 103. It was the one we had chosen from the plan!! So we moved there in January 2017. That flat was pure gold provision.....

TRAFFIC MIRACLE

One morning in early 2018 we were slowly crawling along in a queue of traffic towards Spitals roundabout, Huntingdon, travelling east/west on our way to visit my grandson Chris in Northamptonshire. We needed to get to see him before he left for work at 1.30 pm.

About 100 yards from the roundabout, traffic came to a complete standstill. It became apparent that we were not going to be making further progress any time soon.

We were in the outside lane in the car with large lorries on my left, in front and behind us; we were completely boxed in. On the roundabout just ahead huge lorries were at a standstill.

Nothing was moving. I telephoned the police to see if it had been reported. I was told there was a serious accident somewhere further down on the A14 going towards Cambridge some 15 miles away and they asked for patience, but it would be some hours before it could be cleared. They were doing their best. It would not be likely to move for a long time. What could be done? We were stuck......

Quick arrow prayer. "Lord please can you get us out of this one?" (or something to that effect) "You are the Lord of traffic and everything.....could you please move this so we can get through?" Suddenly to my left a gap appeared in the traffic; I hadn't even noticed any movement. One lorry stayed back and a couple of vehicles moved further up - I don't know how. On the roundabout a small gap round a lorry appeared on the far westbound side.

It took a few seconds for me to realise that there was space and maybe I could get through it so I moved over to the left in the gap and then there was another gap on the right. I moved round and zigzagged in and out of the stationary traffic to the roundabout. The lorry immediately in front of me was completely blocking but then I moved around it to the right and then to the left. A small gap appeared in the south-going traffic on the roundabout. I could get through that lane to the far lane to join the westbound traffic round the roundabout and then onto the A14 going west which was clear.

"Thank you Lord!"

We heard later on the radio that the blockage on the A14 going south continued for some hours and I still don't know how we managed to get through. It had to be God who could move vehicles when the police couldn't! After all if He can move mountains, it's not difficult for him to move traffic because it's got wheels.........!

I know that God also cared about all the other people stuck in that traffic jam......and those involved in the accident........but maybe they just didn't ask?

PARKING TICKET

In early spring 2018 whilst living in St. Ives, Cambridgeshire, we had popped in to Sainsbury's in Huntingdon to do a bit of shopping and also have a cup of tea.

Due to Bob's Alzheimers we had a blue badge enabling us to park in disabled spaces. This made our lives so much easier when shopping and coping with a confused husband who didn't always understand even the simplest instruction like "get out of the car" ...."please would you get out of the car". "Bob darling, we really need to get out of the car".

So it was not surprising on that occasion that in all the hassle, although I had parked on a blue badge space, I forgot to put the badge in the windscreen.

We went into the café, and were just queuing for our tea when I spotted through the window the parking attendant about to write a ticket. It was too late to rush outside and try to stop him.

"Oh no......" I thought, then, not even a prayer, just a further thought flitted through my mind. "Maybe he'll write the wrong registration number on the ticket."

The yellow and black plastic bag containing the incriminating document was stuck firmly to the windscreen. There was no point in going straight outside......the awful deed was done, so we carried on with tea and shopping.

When we got outside I removed the bag from the windscreen and opened it.

What had just been a thought, proved to be true. The parking attendant had printed the registration number of the car incorrectly, therefore the penalty was invalid!

This set me wondering....at what point do thoughts become prayers and prayers become thoughts? He knows all our thoughts anyway – there is nothing that we can hide from him and he works EVERYTHING together for our good when we trust him.

JOE AND THE GAME OF RUMMY

J oe loved a game of Rummy. I think there are many different versions of the game, but whenever we got together as a family, we always played what the rest of us called 'Joe's Rummy'. Joe was my son-in-law's father, and he had his own unique rules, which the rest of us had to obey.

Whenever we spent any time with Joe, we always had to play the game and most importantly, family Christmases were dominated by a group of us getting together round the dining table while Joe held sway to make sure we all obeyed the rules. He himself was an expert at the game and he also had to follow his unique system of scoring. This seemed so complicated to the rest of us as we often had to wait for him to do the maths when we had been playing for several hours because the figures stretched in long columns to the bottom of a lengthy page!

I really don't know what triggered it and certainly don't remember a particularly spiritual conversation leading to it, but one Boxing Day, I think about 2015, five of us, Joe, his son Clive, my son David, Bob and I, were enjoying our usual game of rummy, heads down, deep in concentration, when Joe suddenly looked up from his hand of cards, and straight across the table at me.

His question came right 'out of the blue' and surprised us all.

"How can I know I'm going to heaven when I die?" The question hung there for a few seconds while we absorbed the importance of it.

David said, "Let's finish this game then we'll talk about it......."

"No," I said, "this is too important. Let's lay the cards down and talk about it now".

We each laid our hand of cards face down, in fan-like order.

I explained that Jesus had come into the world, the only perfect and sinless man who ever lived, in order to die on the cross so that he could take our sins on himself and so that we could be forgiven and go to be with him in heaven.

"Do you believe that Joe?"

"Yes I do".

"Then we have to ask him to forgive us for everything we have ever done wrong and invite him to come into our lives and receive him as our Lord and Saviour. Have you ever done that Joe?"

"No I haven't."

"Would you like to?"

"Yes I would", said Joe..

"Then let's all pray together. I'll pray and you repeat after me".

I then prayed the following bite size sentences and each of the others in the room followed, praying out loud……..

"Dear Lord Jesus……………..
Murmured responses took place from all round the table.

"Thank you for coming into the world to die on the cross……….

"so that I might be forgiven…………..

"please forgive me for all that I have ever done wrong………."
The responses continued.

"Please come into my life and be my Lord and Saviour………

"and fill me with your Holy Spirit………..

"Amen............"

And after a resounding echo of an "Amen" we simply picked up the cards and continued the game of rummy where we'd left off.

I had a sense of unreality following this, thinking, "Did that really happen? Was that real?"

But yes it was, because as Joe was leaving to go home he asked if I would write out the words of the prayer I had prayed so that he could have them.

There were a number of other conversations and prayers that took place with Joe over the next few years right up to the day he finally lost consciousness at the age of 93 in September 2019. In one of these the Spirit of God prompted me to say a few more words to him by way of comfort. We had had several conversations about his fear of dying, and so I asked my son-in-law's permission to have a special talk with him. His eyes remained closed during the whole time and he was not able to speak, only to nod his head by way of affirmation.

"Joe" I said. "Do you remember when you lived in Kisumu (Kenya) and you went out to work every day?" He nodded.

"And when you came home each evening, Agnes would be there to greet you with open arms and she would give you a great big hug?" Again the nod (no one had told me about this scenario, except the Holy Spirit of God).

"And it was so lovely to be home again?" Joe nodded affirmation.

"That is what dying is like Joe. It's like going home, tired and weary but Jesus will be waiting there with his arms wide open to greet you with a great big hug......and Agnes will be there too and all the people who know and love Jesus". He nodded and there was peace on his face.

Soon after that he lost consciousness until he died peacefully a few days later......

FLU JAB
TRAFFIC JAM

One Saturday in September 2019 I had an appointment at 10 a.m. at my GP Surgery for my annual 'flu' vaccination. Nothing remarkable about that. Turn up, roll up sleeve, take my turn in the queue while the 'jab' took place. Usually several people would be booked at the same time and you moved through like a conveyor system.

Even allowing for the normal sit and wait in the waiting room afterwards to see there were no adverse reactions, I reckoned that I'd be through and back home by 10.30 in time to meet two friends for coffee at the Kairos coffee shop opposite where I now live in Solihull.

.........So much for good intentions and planning! As I set off in my car for the half mile or so journey to the surgery, I thought I was in plenty of time to get there for the appointment. Halfway along the road, the traffic came to a standstill. We moved slowly along, a few cars at a time, as changing traffic lights at the far end of the road allowed brief movement.

By the time I reached the entrance to the road where stood the surgery, I realised I was well late. To my surprise there were two people in yellow high viz jackets controlling cars entering and leaving the road, and it was blocked all the way to the entrance to the surgery car park. More yellow jackets directing traffic! I wound down my car window to speak to one of them.

"What's the problem," I asked. "Has there been an accident?"

"No," was the reply. "It's just that the two surgeries next door to each other are both holding 'flu' vaccination clinics this morning!"

Ridiculous! A traffic jam caused by a 'flu' jab clinic?!!! I knew that even if I managed to drive into the car park there would be nowhere to park. A brief break in the traffic coming from the opposite direction enabled me to turn around with a seven point turn in that narrow road.

Oh well, I'd just have to rebook at a less busy time. My two friends waiting for me were more important!

My Irish friend Margaret was staying with me for a few days, breaking her journey from Texas via Birmingham on her way to Ireland, so I wanted to make the most of every minute with her.

We met up with Pam in Kairos coffee shop where we all talked animatedly for more than an hour.

After lunch, Margaret said she also needed to get her 'flu' vaccination done and we wondered if this would be possible that same day in one of the local Pharmacies where the service was on offer.

I rang several, but only one was able to carry it out that afternoon. Margaret was leaving the country in two days.

We duly went along after lunch where we had the ministrations of a lovely lady in an otherwise empty shop!

I went in first and somehow during the course of the form filling, consent, etc. she asked me what I do with my time, so we got round to the subject of the writing of the stories in this book. She asked me to tell her one of the stories so I briefly re-counted the story in chapter one.

We talked about God and she said that she be-lieved we were meant to meet that day and would like to read the book when it is finished. I made a note of her name.

The river took an unexpected turn that day, with a little sparkle of gold in it!

THE LORD IS
MY OPTICIAN

I had my eyes tested last week. Nothing unusual about that. It's now the end of 2019. I have had annual eye tests most of my life, due to the fact that both my mother and her father, my grandfather, had had glaucoma which always qualified me for free annual tests.

More than 35 year ago, my eye sight had seemed to be deteriorating with an optician prescribing glasses for me to improve my sight for reading and watching television. He predicted, "In ten years' time, you will be wearing glasses all the time".

That was the prognosis, "......but Lord, you are in control of my life and I do not accept that prognosis".

My eyesight was especially valued by me because my mother and her sister had been born with imperfect sight and both had been completely blind for the last years of their lives.

So I have had my regular checkups. I have had reading glasses prescribed in the past to improve reading and driving sight, but have seldom worn them. Each time I have attended for my eye tests the optician has declared "There's no change - your eyes have not changed since last year."

So I am still praising and thanking God for his goodness to me in keeping me free of the need for glasses, I sometimes wear my driving glasses to rest my eyes from glare, but I remain legal to drive without them.

MAGISTRATES COURT

The Court Room was hushed; everyone stood to wait while the magistrates left the room to consider their verdict.

Corrine (not her real name) and I stood together at the back, talking. She was in panic mode. "I'm going down.... I'm going down, I know I am. Tell mum to take care of the children for me."

I tried to calm her reminding her that we had not yet heard the verdict, but my words had little effect as she already had a suspended sentence which by further offences was now broken and she knew that she rightly deserved a prison sentence.

I had driven with her from Essex to Kent for the Court hearing. She was a young mother, a single parent, with a track record of offences and already with a suspended sentence hanging over her.

The case had been adjourned several times already but this time I was privileged to be taking Corrine along myself. She had recently started to attend the church I was part of and had met with Jesus and given her life into his hands. As we had driven across the River Thames that morning, we had been praying and committing the court case into God's hands and asking for a Solicitor to represent her who would be the right one to represent her case to the Court.

Corrine knew that she was guilty of the offences she was accused of and had begun to see her guilt from a different perspective knowing that now God had forgiven her for the whole of a very messed up life, and that he wanted the best for her.

When we had arrived at the Court we were ushered into an anteroom and introduced to a very nice man who listened to Corrine's story, of her guilt, but also that she now had become a Christian and wanted to live a renewed and reformed life. We discovered to our wonder that he was a Christian.

When we went into the Courtroom, there were three magistrates and several witnesses Two of whom were floor walkers in the store where Corrine had been seen shoplifting and putting a number of items deliberately into her shopping bag. They each gave their evidence and clearly, they felt they had got her nailed as she was unquestionably guilty of the crimes of which she was accused.

Then the defence Solicitor rose to his feet and gave a wonderful plea on Corrine's behalf. I only wish that I had a copy of what he said. Instead of attempting to plead her innocence he acknowledged her guilt but pleaded for the magistrates to grant her mercy on the basis of a changed life, instead of judgement. It was a very eloquent speech and must have confounded the floor walkers, who really felt they had nailed her.

As the three magistrates returned, the whole Court reassembled in their original places and Corrine waited trembling for the sentence she knew she deserved.

They agreed to indeed grant her mercy and gave her a two-year suspended sentence on top of the suspended sentence already held which was now broken!!! This was almost unheard of as she already deserved a prison sentence.

This so gave a picture of what Jesus has done for us but without a suspended sentence!

The floor walkers represented what the enemy

(Satan) does for us. He is our accuser and we are guilty before God of many sins and broken laws of God. But Jesus (represented by the defending Solicitor) pleads on our behalf and asks for mercy instead of the judgement which we clearly deserve. God (represented by the magistrates) gives us mercy instead of judgement. It is an imperfect and inadequate picture of all that our forgiveness means which is won for us by Jesus on the cross, but at the time, it so represented our freedom as Christians. Imperfect people redeemed by Christ.

Corrine and I were just singing and praising God all the way home in the car because she was free...... She had expected to be taken off to a prison cell but instead she was free to go home to her children.

My compilation of stories was almost ready for me to submit for publishing, but this one story I had been wondering and praying about whether or not to include.

Just this evening, February 2020, I had an unexpected telephone call from Corrine whom I had not had any contact with for some years, which led to our remembering all the above which happened in the late 1980's and all that that event had accomplished in her life. She admitted to not having lived a perfect life (who has?) but she has kept on the straight and narrow and never broken the law again leading to that suspended sentence coming into operation. She has held down a responsible job for many years and been a good mother to her children. She still knows the love of God in her life and knows without Him, there could have been a very different story.

I have written this with Corrine's permission.

ANOTHER BEND IN THE RIVER!

In June 2018, we moved yet again. I can't say this one was clearly led by God, but I believe that He works all things together for our good. It has been the hardest time because Bob's Alzheimer's Disease, now into its thirteenth year, has meant needing more help and support and we moved mainly to be close to daughter Pauline in Solihull. And for her benefit because we had had several crises involving her driving 85 miles to get to us in emergency situations.

The first was my breast cancer in 2013, involving two operations, one for mastectomy and another for lymph node removal. I dislocated my shoulder in late 2014 while barn dancing at a wedding, necessitating a drive over from Solihull during the night by Pauline and Des, then six weeks later I broke my neck of femur and had it pinned and hip replacement. In June 2017, Bob was hospitalised with sepsis and Pauline arrived at the hospital all the way from Solihull before we got there.

Bob now has dysphagia (difficulty swallowing) and has mostly lost his power of speech. Although sometimes he talks animatedly it is mostly unintelligible. On rare occasions some little gem of a sentence will come out and when that happens I know such joy, similar to the joy a parent experiences when a small child says their first words!!! He still recognises me and Pauline.

We moved into extra care flats, but Bob objected to the carers helping him and it was getting to be difficult for me to cope with him on my own. In December 2018, the very painful decision was made that he should go into a care home although I had always hoped to be able to keep him with me for the rest of his life.

I visit him there every day. I still see a wonderful man who looks just the same as he ever did, but there's grieving also for what he used to be. There is still much gold in the river - he is still loving and caring and I love to be with him more than anyone in the world. I pray for him and with him regularly and he still knows and understands prayer. And I know that one day, in heaven there will be no more tears, no more sorrow no more suffering and no more separation...........come Lord Jesus and restore this world and all its suffering and sickness to what you died to make possible. Meanwhile I am still looking for the gold in the river of life.

One absolute nugget, is that since moving here I have met two wonderful friends, Pam and Mike. Mike has just written and published a book and he has helped and encouraged me to get this book written and published, so in spite of the grit and grime of life, I have found more gold.

Also some friends in the church house group I attend have been very prophetic and encouraging. My writing had been going very slowly. In the summer of 2019 I only had six of these stories/chapters written. One prophetic picture that was given to me made me jump when the lady who gave it suddenly said "I see you taking the reins of a horse, and galloping!" I knew it related to the writing of this book. During the following two weeks, I took the reins and wrote thirty more stories! It was a supernatural experience during that time. Each step of it has been guided when I have waited not knowing the way forward.

About Jesus' earthly life, it is written in the Bible in John chapter 21 verse 25 - 'Jesus also did many other things. If they were all written down I suppose the whole world could not contain the books that would be written.'

Because Jesus is still alive today by his Spirit, he is still doing the same things in the lives of his followers that he did when he was a man living on earth. If all the things he is still doing and has been doing for the last two thousand years, were written in books then even the whole universe would not contain them! Mine is just a small portion of those things I have seen him do in my lifetime.

So this is an ongoing story......I am looking forward to seeing where the river goes next......!!!!

If you would like to contact me with your comments on anything I have written, or even have a personal 'God Story' you would like to share with me, then please email me on jfwgoldriver@mail.com

Printed in Poland
by Amazon Fulfillment
Poland Sp. z o.o., Wrocław

54732588R00116